Dedalus European Classics
General Editor: Mike Mitchell

Parisian Sketches

Jean-Louis Forain, *La Maison Close*. This etching, originally commissioned for the first edition of *Croquis parisiens* (1880), was one of two that were eventually excluded from the published version.

J.-K. Huysmans

Parisian Sketches

Translated and with an introduction
and notes by Brendan King

Dedalus

Dedalus would like to thank Grants for the Arts for its assistance in producing this book.

ARTS COUNCIL ENGLAND

LOTTERY FUNDED

Published in the UK by Dedalus Ltd, Langford Lodge,
St Judith's Lane, Sawtry, Cambs, PE28 5XE
email: DedalusLimited@compuserve.com
www: dedalusbooks.com

ISBN 1 903517 24 9

Dedalus is distributed in the United States by SCB Distributors,
15608 South New Century Drive, Gardena, California 90248
email: info@scbdistributors.com   web site: www.scbdistributors.com

Dedalus is distributed in Australia & New Zealand by Peribo Pty Ltd.
58 Beaumont Road, Mount Kuring-gai N.S.W. 2080
email: peribo@bigpond.com

Dedalus is distributed in Canada by Marginal Distribution,
695, Westney Road South, Suite 14 Ajax, Ontario, L16 6M9
email: marginal@marginalbook.com   web site: www.marginalbook.com

First published in France in 1880
First published by Dedalus in 2004

The Introduction, notes and translation copyright © Brendan King 2004

The right of Brendan King to be identified as the translator of this work has been asserted by him in accordance with the Copyright, Designs and Patent Act, 1988.

Printed in Finland by WS Bookwell
Typeset by RefineCatch Ltd, Bungay, Suffolk

THE TRANSLATOR

Brendan King is a freelance writer, reviewer and translator with a special interest in late nineteenth-century French fiction.

He is currently working on a Ph.D. on the life and work of J.-K. Huysmans. His translations include *Là-Bas* by J.-K. Huysmans published by Dedalus in 2001.

He lives on the Isle of Wight.

CONTENTS

CONTENTS

INTRODUCTION

When *Croquis parisiens* (*Parisian Sketches*) was first
published in 1880, J.-K. Huysmans was in the process
of establishing a reputation for himself as a formidable force within the Naturalist school, a group of
younger writers with common literary interests who
acknowledged Emile Zola as their head. At 32,
Huysmans must have felt that he was finally starting
to make his mark on the Parisian literary scene after
something of a slow start. His first book, a collection
of prose poems entitled *Le Drageoir à épices* (1874),
had to be published at his own expense, and though
it attracted a little critical attention, its sales were
negligible. His first novel, *Marthe, histoire d'une fille*
(1876), had an equally inauspicious start: after
arranging to have the book printed in Belgium,
Huysmans was stopped by customs at the French
border and nearly 400 copies were impounded to pre-
vent 'an outrage on public morals'. However, enough
got through to allow him to send complimentary
copies to the writers he most admired, and the book
effectively served as an entrée to both Edmond de
Goncourt's *grenier* and Zola's Thursday evening literary gatherings. With the contacts he subsequently
made through them, his writing career quickly took
off: his work began to appear in numerous journals,
both in Paris and Belgium, and his second novel, *Les*

Soeurs Vatard (1879), was accepted by Charpentier, Zola's own publisher. The novel, which included a dedication to Zola from 'his fervent admirer and devoted friend', was a *succès de scandale* and attracted a huge amount of press coverage that inextricably linked his name with that of Zola's in the public mind. When, early the following year, his short story 'Sac au dos' was included in *Les Soirées de Médan*, a collection of six novellas written by Zola and five of his Naturalist 'disciples', including Guy de Maupassant, Léon Hennique and Huysmans himself, his place in the movement seemed assured.

But Naturalism's refusal to idealise human existence, its insistence that life was subject to inexorable laws of heredity and social conditioning, ensured that it would never find an easy acceptance, either with the public or the conservative press. By 1880, it had become a contentious subject of public debate; the battle lines were drawn, and many of those in the literary press saw the spread of the movement as something that was neither morally healthy or socially desirable. To his critics, Huysmans' work was, if anything, an even more virulent strain of the new literary disease than that they detected in Zola's 'pornographic' and 'putrid' writings. Outraged reviewers of *Les Soeurs Vatard* complained that he out-Zola'd Zola in his willingness to rub his readers' noses in the more sordid aspects of contemporary Parisian life:

> Emile Zola has produced a school, but as the disciples of the master can't equal him in talent,

they have surpassed him in extravagant obscenities, in Naturalistic ravings.

(*Polybiblion Revue Bibliographique. Universelle*, October 1880)

Another contemporary reviewer of the same book fulminated against the crudity of Huysmans' descriptions, and his attitude sums up much of the conservative reaction to the graphic nature of Naturalist realism:

Every time the author talks about a pair of boots, they're oozing and smelling; in describing a gathering of the fairer sex, Monsieur Huysmans tells us about the ladies' sweat, which recalls 'the strong fragrance of goats frolicking in the sun', and then concludes by saying that these odours were mixed with 'whiffs of tainted pig-meat and wine, with the acrid stink of cats' piss and the rude stench of the latrine . . .'! That's all very well, but I prefer something else.

(*L'Evenement*, 23 March 1879)

Yet contrary to the common perception among those in the press, Huysmans was not a typical Naturalist – in reality his work was both stylistically and formally at odds with some of the core tenets of the movement – and *Parisian Sketches*, published just a year after *Les Soeurs Vatard*, was in no way a work typical of the Naturalist school. In spite of its documentary attention to the details of everyday life, one of the characteristics of Naturalist prose, its literary and stylistic exuberance, its idiosyncratic view of Paris and Parisians, and its fascination with the fantastic and the exotic, show that Zola's brand of Naturalism could never have contained Huysmans for long. Even Zola seemed to recognise as much when he reviewed the book in 1880:

> He [Huysmans] is one of boldest, most unpredictable, most intense virtuosos of language. He has written pages in which Rubens' village fairs, overflowing with activity, come alive, pages created with a palette of colours and a peculiarity of design that are absolutely original, such as one doesn't find anywhere else. Really, it's stupid to think that such a gifted writer needed to attach himself to what has so foolishly been called the Naturalist school in order to make his way in the literary world through shameless pastiche. He was fully formed as a writer when we first met and had already given the measure of his power in pages that were published all over the place . . .
>
> (Emile Zola, *La Voltaire*, 15 June 1880)

But if Zola read the signs, he certainly did not understand them and a few years later when Huysmans dropped his literary bombshell, *A Rebours*, the novel that not only radically altered the public's perception of him as a writer, but also changed the literary landscape of *fin-de-siècle* France, it seems to have caught Zola unawares. After reading the book, he sent Huysmans a long letter criticising the book piecemeal and ended with the misguided and dismissive prophecy that 'at least it would count as a curiosity among your other works' (Letter from Emile Zola, 20 May 1884). As extravagant a departure from the Naturalist path as it seemed to Zola at the time, with its decadent, aristocratic anti-hero who turns his back on the modern world the Naturalists were attempting to critique, *A Rebours* did not in fact spring fully-formed out of nowhere. As Jennifer Birkett has pointed out, it is possible to see in *Parisian Sketches*, in embryonic form, many of the themes, motifs and obsessions that would later resurface in Huysmans' most famous work:

> *Croquis parisiens*, illustrated with engravings by Forain and Raffaëlli, is a clear prelude to *A Rebours*. The model is Baudelaire transforming the sordid landscape of the modern city with fleeting glimpses of perverse beauty. Grotesque details plucked out from the whole, intensified to dreamlike proportions, turn ugliness into a source of pleasure.
>
> (Jennifer Birkett, *The Sins of the Fathers*, Quartet, 1986)

Parisian Sketches may be a prologue to *A Rebours*, but it is also much more than that. Although the first edition of the book appeared in 1880, four years before Huysmans' decadent masterpiece, the second edition, revised and expanded with the addition of seven new pieces, was published two years after it, in

1886. In that space of time Huysmans had gone from being the rising star of the Naturalist movement to the man who had dealt it a death blow, and this shift is reflected both in the form of the 'sketches' themselves and in the changing narrative viewpoint as the book progresses. The book's opening sketch, 'The Folies-Bergère in 1879', vivid and expressive though it is, conforms to many of the conventions of realist prose. In it, Huysmans describes a world that seems to exist physically and objectively, independent of the observer or his state of mind. By contrast, the final pieces in the collection, such as 'Nightmare' and 'The Overture to *Tannhäuser*', are written in an allusive style that was to become typical of the Symbolists, a style that attempts to express the feelings and sensations that lie beyond everyday awareness. These virtuoso sketches present a world of subjective impressions, one experienced almost wholly through the individual consciousness of their narrators.

With its six-year gestation period and the inclusion of material that spanned over a decade, *Parisian Sketches* embodies the transition from Huysmans' youthful literary interests to the later preoccupations of his mature period. It simultaneously harks back to the prose poems of Charles Baudelaire and Aloysius Bertrand, and anticipates the Decadent and Symbolist movements of the late 1880s and early 1890s; it points forward to *A Rebours*, but it also points beyond it, to the aesthetic theory Huysmans would later expound under the name of 'spiritual naturalism' in *Là-Bas* (1891), his novel of contemporary Parisian occultism.

Parisian Sketches: the art of writing

Huysmans' lifelong passion for art was reflected in his writing: his novels, short stories and prose poems are studded with references to specific paintings and artists, and emblematic 'transpositions d'art', such as those of Gustave Moreau's *Salomé* in *A Rebours* and Matthias Grünewald's *Crucifixion* in *Là-bas*, are a recurrent feature of his work. Although many writers of the time were also preoccupied with art, this obsession with the image was to a large degree conditioned by the particular circumstances of his childhood. His Dutch-born father, Victor, like his father before him, was an artist by profession and traced his ancestry back to Cornelius Huysmans, one of whose canvases hung in the Louvre. Huysmans was greatly affected by his father's early death in 1856 and by his mother's subsequent marriage just a year later to a man he disliked, and it is possible to see in his later adoption of the Dutch form of two of his Christian names (he was baptised Charles-Marie-Georges, but changed his name to Joris-Karl on the title page of his first book), as well as in his self-conscious insistence on his Dutch, painterly heritage, the expression of an oedipal desire to assume his father's identity.

Huysmans wrote on more than one occasion that he wanted to do with the pen what great artists had done with the brush, and this theme was reiterated throughout his early work: his first major commission as a journalist was a series of descriptive pieces to be printed under the heading 'Croquis et eaux-fortes'

(Sketches and Etchings); his first collection of prose poems, *Le Drageoir à épices*, included an introductory sonnet that described the book's contents as a 'selection of faded pastels, etchings and old prints'; and with *Parisian Sketches* he made the metaphorical parallel between writing and art explicit, his punning title alluding to Honoré Daumier's popular series of cartoons and sketches that had been published in *Le Charivari* throughout the 1840s, 50s and 60s under the title *Croquis parisiens*. (When he came to illustrate Huysmans' story 'The Streetwalker', Jean-Louis Forain offered his own *hommage* to Daumier by adapting and updating his famous sketch on the theme of '*Coquetterie*'.)

Like any collection of prints collected over a period of time, *Parisian Sketches*, which includes work written between 1874 and 1885, can be divided into 'periods' in which the influence of a particular artist or artistic movement can be traced. In the sketches written prior to 1876, the year in which Huysmans first encountered the work of Edgar Degas, the intimist spirit of the Dutch painters of the seventeenth century for whom Huysmans had a profound attachment seems to be to the fore; in those written between 1876 and 1880, it is Degas' concert-hall paintings and the urban landscapes of the Impressionists that dominate the writer's visual imagination; and in the final pieces of the book there is a noticeable shift away from the representation of the objective world and an increasing focus on subjective perception, in sketches that are directly inspired by the internalised mindscapes of Odilon Redon.

Huysmans' discovery of Degas' work in an exhibition of 1876 marked a turning point in the development of his ideas about art and representation. In his subsequent art criticism, a volume of which was published under the title *L'Art Moderne* in 1883, midway between the two editions of *Parisian Sketches*, Huysmans launched a series of vitriolic attacks on academic painting and the conventional art of the Salon: 'Let's have art that lives and breathes, for God's sake,' he wrote, 'and into the bin with all the cardboard goddesses and devotional junk of the past!' Like the Naturalists, the early Impressionists were more often reviled than praised for their innovations, but Huysmans was a fervent advocate of their cause and set about establishing Impressionism as a new artistic paradigm: 'It is to the small group of Impressionists,' he wrote in his account of the 'Exposition des Indépendants' of 1880, 'that the honour belongs for having swept away all the prejudices, for having overturned all the old conventions of art.' His review concluded with a rhetorical flourish, asking how long it would be before Degas was recognised as the 'greatest painter we have in France today'.

The extent to which Huysmans was influenced by the Impressionists in general and Degas in particular can be gauged from the first four sections of *Parisian Sketches*. It is impossible now to read such pieces as 'The Folies-Bergère in 1879', 'Dance night at the Brasserie Européenne in Grenelle', 'The Streetwalker' and 'View of the ramparts of north Paris' without being reminded of Impressionist paintings that have reached an almost iconic status through mass reproduction: Degas' *Miss La-La at the Cirque Fernando*, Manet's *Bar at the Folies-Bergère*, Renoir's *Ball at the Moulin de Galette*, Caillebotte's *On the Europe Bridge*, Monet's *Gare Saint-Lazare*, and numerous others.

When he came to look for illustrators for *Parisian Sketches*, it was almost inevitable that Huysmans would turn to two artists who were closely associated with the Impressionist movement and whom he had praised extravagantly in his Salon reviews: Jean-Louis Forain (a former student of Degas' who had already provided a frontispiece for the 1879 edition of Huysmans' first novel, *Marthe, histoire d'une fille*) and Jean-François Raffaëlli. Both men had distinguished themselves with their etchings, a medium that was more easily reproduced in book form than Degas' colour pastels, and the first edition of *Parisian Sketches* included eight plates, four by each artist.

Forain and Raffaëlli were ideal illustrators for Huysmans' work, their contrasting styles and subject matter perfectly complementing the diverse aspects of Paris that so attracted him. Raffaëlli tended to concentrate on scenes of poverty and neglect, and his landscapes of areas such as the Bièvre and his portraits of destitute or working class Parisians echoed Huysmans' fascination with suburban decay. By contrast, Forain's theme was the twin strand of elegance and vice that ran through fashionable Parisian life, and his work focused more on character and the nuances of social situations.

Huysmans' enthusiasm for the Impressionists did

not blind him to other artists, even if their work was antithetical to its ideas, and if Degas' spirit hovers over the opening sections of *Parisian Sketches*, that of Odilon Redon hovers over its close. Huysmans had first seen Redon's distinctive charcoal drawings in an exhibition at the offices of *La Vie Moderne* in 1881, and the following year he wrote to the artist asking where he could buy prints from the collection *Dans le Rêve*, after seeing an edition belonging to his editor, Charpentier. Within a short time the two men became close friends, and Redon later recalled that Huysmans 'always felt at home' with them during his regular visits to the artist and his wife. Perhaps the defining moment in their friendship was the prose poem Huysmans wrote in February 1885, inspired by Redon's limited edition set of six etchings, *Hommage à Goya*. Published first in the *Revue Indépendant*, it was reprinted in the 1886 edition of *Parisian Sketches* with only slight changes, under the title 'Cauchemar' (Nightmare). Brilliant though Huysmans' evocations of Redon's prints are, it must have piqued the artist to see his work adapted and presented – not to say misrepresented – through the medium of another man's words. Certainly 'Cauchemar' reveals more about Huysmans the writer than it does about Redon the artist, and it was as a result of this kind of literary 'appropriation' – exacerbated in 1889 by the publication of Huysmans' second volume of art criticism, *Certains*, in which he implicated Redon in his own growing fascination with Satanism and the occult – that the two men's friendship began to cool off by the end of the decade.

INTRODUCTION

Huysmans: flâneur parisien

Amid the popular images of Huysmans the Decadent, Huysmans the Satanist, or even Huysmans the Monk, it is easy to forget that, like his hero Baudelaire, Huysmans was a *flâneur parisien*, a habitual walker of the city's back streets and byways, a prose poet of its forgotten corners and neglected alleyways. Particular areas of the city seemed to have a symbolic resonance for him and this was reflected in almost every page of his work, whether in the fictionalised peregrinations of his characters through the city's streets, in journalistic travelogues such as 'A travers le Jardin du Luxembourg', 'Le Parc Monceau' and 'Autour des fortifications', or in extended studies of particular *quartiers*, such as *La Bièvre* (1890) and *Le Quartier Notre-Dame* (1905). It has been said of Huysmans' Paris what was once said of James Joyce's Dublin: that if his native city were to be demolished overnight, it could be rebuilt down to the last brick using his works as a guide. When Walter Benjamin was assembling *The Arcades Project*, his kaleidoscopic source book to the city he called 'the capital of the nineteenth century', he included several lengthy extracts from Huysmans' descriptions of Paris, all of which were drawn from *Parisian Sketches*. Huysmans was one of the great nineteenth century writers on Paris, and *Parisian Sketches*, with its stunning evocation of the city's streets, its people, its sights and its smells, is a literary *tour-de-force* inspired by the capital in which he was born and in which he lived almost the whole of his life.

Huysmans was a *flâneur*, but he was a *flâneur à rebours* who was almost wilfully perverse in the choice of locations he explored. He had an especial fondness for the Bièvre and its surroundings, the pestilential river that had long since become a byword for decay and neglect, as well as the insalubrious districts around Saint-Séverin and Place Maubert. It was here, in some of the lowest haunts in Paris, that he observed the drunkards, prostitutes and petty criminals who would eventually find their way into *Parisian Sketches*. Such expeditions had their risks: in a book recalling his walks with Huysmans, Michel de Lezinier describes how some years before, those who tried to trace the course of the Bièvre's slimy waters through the slums of Paris, armed with their cameras and notebooks, had been attacked and set on by suspicious residents.

Despite the scenes of urban poverty against which Huysmans the *flâneur* chose to set his sketches, it was the aesthetic, not the social, aspect of the experience he was interested in. Unlike Zola, who often sought to make political capital out of social injustice or economic distress in his novels, Huysmans' prose poems aestheticise their subjects rather than politicise them. His need to paint the world with words, his obsessive attention to detail and his desire to fix what he saw in a satisfying artistic form, can all be seen as strategies, if not to impose order on what he saw as threatening elements within society, then at least to contain them or keep them at arm's length.

Huysmans' views about the poorer *quartiers* of Paris have to be seen in the context of his experience of the Paris Commune, the most violent outbreak of revolutionary activity in nineteenth-century France. As an employee in the Ministry of the Interior, Huysmans had spent the months of the Commune exiled in Versailles, where the government had moved after the capitulation of Paris to the Prussians in 1870. He saw nothing of the terrible drama of revolution and civil war as it was enacted in Paris during the April and May of 1871, but he had to spend a few days in Paris on official business in June, and came back sickened by the stories of carnage he heard and aghast at the damage that had been inflicted on the city. As a consequence, the sight of working class poverty was forever associated with the threat of social rebellion: in 'The Bièvre' even a red cotton eiderdown, hanging from a window in a run-down quarter by the river, ominously 'sounds a piercing note like a call to arms'. Although Huysmans feared the threat to social order posed by a disenfranchised working class, he also detested the mediocrity and complacency of the *bourgeois* who kept the system in place. Huysmans' contempt for the middle class and distaste for the working class left him no place to go, and perhaps this explains the attraction for him of various forms of 'elite' communities, whether the intellectual elitism of the bibliophile, the Satanic elitism of the occult initiate, or the monastic elite of a religious order.

As a record of a vanished culture, *Parisian Sketches* is a rich sociological and cultural archive that can be endlessly mined, and one that can be read on several different levels: as travelogue, as social history, as literature, as autobiography. As acute as Huysmans' social observations are, and as vibrant as his evocations of Parisian life can be, however, it is not just the historical Paris that is revealed in the diverse texts he presents us with: if the seven sections into which *Parisian Sketches* is divided constitute an extended *flânerie*, it is a journey that not only maps the physical contours of the city of light, of Benjamin's 'capital of the nineteenth century', but one that also maps the metaphysical contours of its author's complex psyche, a writer who once described himself as an 'inexplicable cross between a refined Parisian and a Dutch painter'.

A note on the translation

Surprisingly, there is no critical edition of *Croquis parisiens* available in French, though Lucien Descaves did provide some brief annotations to the text in his edition of the *Oeuvres complètes*, published by Crès between 1928 and 1934. The text printed in that edition is the one that has been used for this translation. An English translation by Richard Griffiths, containing a helpful introduction and notes, was published by the Fortune Press in 1962, but it has long since been out of print. As many have previously remarked with regard to Huysmans, he is a difficult writer to render faithfully in English: he was a frequent coiner of neologisms and his books are scattered with obscure words, archaisms, and references to now-forgotten incidents. *Parisian Sketches* is no exception. It would of course be impossible to provide footnotes for every uncommon usage or for every word belonging to a specialised vocabulary, however I have attempted to include explanations and definitions to those which don't appear in the average dictionary, as well as providing more comprehensive critical notes designed to elucidate references in the text that might otherwise remain unclear. To avoid distracting the reader with obtrusive footnotes, the notes have been placed at the back of the book and arranged by section and page number.

Select Bibliography

Not a great deal has been written in English specifically about *Parisian Sketches*. However, listed below are a few books and articles that either provide useful background material on Huysmans' work or explore the book's themes in more depth:

Robert Baldick. *The Life of J.-K. Huysmans*, Oxford at the Clarendon Press, 1955.

Anita Brookner. *The Genius of the Future: Essays in French Art Criticism*. Phaidon Press, 1971.

George A. Cevasco. 'J.-K. Huysmans and the Impressionists.' *Journal of Aesthetics and Art Criticism*, No.17, December 1958.

Leonard R. Koos. 'A River Runs Through It: La Bièvre, Huysmans and Nineteenth-Century Paris.' *French Literature in/and the City*, French Literature Series Volume XXIV, Amsterdam: Rodopi, 1997.

Charles Nunley. 'Huysmans and the Aesthetics of Solitude in *Croquis parisiens*.' *French Forum*, May 1996.

Theodore Reff. *Degas: The Artist's Mind*. Belknap Press, 1987.

Robert Storey. 'Pierrot-Oedipe: J.-K. Huysmans and the Circus-Pantomime.' *French Forum*, January 1981.

PARISIAN SKETCHES

I. THE FOLIES-BERGÈRE IN 1879

Jean-Louis Forain, *Les Folies-Bergère*. One of four original etchings by Forain included in the first edition of *Croquis parisiens* (1880).

I

After you've endured the shouts of programme-sellers and the solicitations of boot-blacks offering to polish your shoes, after you've passed through the ticket-barrier where, standing amid a group of seated gentlemen and assisted by a chain-wearing usher, a young man sporting a ginger moustache, a wooden leg and a red ribbon takes your ticket, the stage curtain finally comes into view, cut across the middle by the ceiling-like mass of the balcony. You can see the lower part of the cloth, and, in front of it, the two grilled eyes of the prompt-boxes and the horse-shoe of an orchestra pit full of heads, an uneven and shifting field where, against the dull gleam of bald heads and the glossy pomaded hair of the men, the hats of the women stand out, their feathers and their flowers sprouting in profusion on all sides.

A great hubbub rises from the gathering crowd. A warm haze, mingled with exhalations of every kind and saturated with the acrid dust that comes from carpets and chairs when you beat them, envelopes the hall. The smell of cigars and women becomes more noticeable; gas lamps, reflected from one end of the theatre to the other by mirrors, burn more dimly;

it is only with difficulty that you can move about, and only with difficulty that you can make out, through the dense ranks of bodies, an acrobat on stage who is methodically devoting himself to some gymnastic exercises on the fixed bar.

For a moment, through a gap formed by two shoulders and two heads, you catch a glimpse of him, bent double, his feet braced and clamped to the bar, accelerating in a circular motion, turning furiously until he loses human form, spitting out sparks like those catherine wheels that whirl round, fizzing, in a shower of gold; then, little by little, the music which has been spinning round with him slows its spiralling pace and, little by little, the form of the acrobat reappears, his pink, gold-braided tights, shaking less energetically now, sparkle only here and there, and then, back on his feet, the man waves to the crowd with both hands.

II

For Ludovic de Francmesnil

Then, as you ascend to the upper gallery of the hall, amid women whose long trains rustle as they snake up the steps, climbing a staircase where the sight of a plaster statue holding a gas-lit torch in its hand immediately reminds you of the entrance of a brothel, the music engulfs you in your turn, feebly at first, then loudly and more distinctly at the next turn of the stairs. A blast of hot air hits you in the face and there, on the landing, you see the opposite sight to that downstairs, a completely reversed image, the curtain falling from the top of the proscenium, cut in the middle by the red ledge of the open boxes curving in half-moons round the balcony suspended a few feet beneath them.

An usherette, her pink ribbons fluttering over a white bonnet, offers you a programme which is a marvel of an art-form that is at once both spiritualist and positivist: phoney Indian cartomancers, a lady who calls herself a palmist and a graphologist, a hypnotist, clairvoyants, soothsayers who tell fortunes using coffee grounds, pianos and ocarinas for hire, job lots of maudlin music for sale, all this for the soul; advertisements for sweets, for corsets and suspenders, radical cures for intimate afflictions, a unique treatment for diseases of the mouth, all this for the body. Only one thing disconcerts: an advert for a sewing machine. It's easy to understand why there's one for a fencing-school, there are a lot of stupid men about! But the 'Silent Wonder' and the 'Singer' aren't tools you ordinarily associate with the working girls who come here; unless this advert was placed here as a symbol of respectability, as an inducement to chaste labours. It is perhaps, under a different form, one of those moral tracts that the English distribute to lead creatures of vice back to virtue.

*   *   *

Imagination is decidedly a very good thing: it allows you to credit people with ideas even more stupid than those they undoubtedly already have.

33

III

For Léon Hennique

They are outrageous and they are magnificent as they march two by two round the semicircular floor of the auditorium, powdered and painted, eyes drowned in a smudge of pale blue, lips ringed in startling red, their breasts thrust out over laced corsets, exuding waves of opoponax which they disperse by fanning, and which mingles with the strong aroma of their underarms and the subtle scent of a flower expiring on their bust.

You watch, entranced, as this gaggle of whores passes rhythmically by, against a dull red backdrop broken only by windows, like wooden merry-go-round horses that twirl in slow-motion to the sound of an organ around a bit of scarlet curtain embellished with mirrors and lamps; you watch their thighs churn under dresses the bottoms of which are edged by white petticoats that flounce, like eddies of foam, under the hem of the material. You gasp as you follow the skill with which these women's backs slide between the bellies of men who, coming in the opposite direction, open and close again around them, revealing a glimpse, through the gaps between the men's heads, of the backs of their chignons, lit on each side by the golden gleam of a piece of jewellery, by the flash of a gemstone.

Then you tire of this interminable round, ceaselessly trodden by the same women, and your ears prick up at the clamour rising from the hall saluting the entrance of the conductor, a tall, thin man known for his revolutionary polkas and for his waltzes. A salvo of applause comes from the promenades above and below the boxes in which suspicious glimpses of white female flesh can be seen amid the shadows. The maestro bows, raises his head with its bristle-brush hair, its greying Chinaman moustache and nose complete with pince-nez, and then, his back turned to the stage, he starts to conduct in his black tails and white tie, calmly stirring the music as if bored or overcome by sleep. Then, all of a sudden, turning towards the brass section, he holds out his baton like a fishing-rod, 'playing' the refrain for all it's worth, extracting the notes with a firm gesture as if pulling out teeth, beating the air up and down, pumping out the end of the melody as one pumps on a beer-pull.

IV

For Paul Daniel

This scrap of music finished, a silence follows and then the clash of a gong reverberates. The curtain rises: the stage is still deserted, but men dressed in grey cotton overalls with red cuffs and collars, are running to all corners of the house, pulling ropes, undoing clamps, adjusting knots. The confusion continues, two or three men rush about on stage, while a superior keeps an eye on them. They ready themselves to stretch an immense net across the middle of the stage and above the orchestra. The net sways, frees itself from the edge of the balcony where it was rolled up, then, running on rings of copper, it jingles like the sea playing with pebbles.

Applause crackles around the hall. The orchestra grinds out a circus waltz; a man and a woman enter wearing flesh-coloured tights, gorgets and Japanese-style shorts, indigo and turquoise blue with silver spangles and fringes. The woman is English, with over-the-top make-up beneath her yellow hair, and an ample behind projecting over her robust thighs; the man is slimmer by comparison, his hair well-groomed, his moustaches curled. The fixed smile of the barber's revolving dummy plays over their scrubbed, Herculean faces. The man leaps onto a rope, hoists himself up to a trapeze that hangs in front of the curtain between two chandeliers, amid the cables and yards up in the roof, and then, sitting on a bar which presses against the flesh of his thighs, he rapidly executes a few manoeuvres, wiping his hands from time to time on a handkerchief attached to one of the cords.

Next, the woman climbs up onto the net, which sags under her weight, and walks across it from one end to the other, bouncing at each step as if on a trampoline, her sulphur-coloured pigtails dancing against her neck in the light. Then, after having climbed on to a small platform suspended over the balcony opposite the man, separated from her by the length of the hall, she waits. All eyes are fixed on her.

Two beams of electric light projected onto her back from the depths of the Folies envelope her, refracting off the curve of her hips, splashing her from neck to feet, gouache-ing her, so to speak, with a silver out-line; then, dividing, they pass separately through the chandeliers, almost invisible as they move, reuniting and spreading out when they reach the man on the trapeze in a fan of bluish light that illuminates the fringes of his mica trunks, sparkling like grains of sugar.

The waltz continues more slowly in gentle, hammock-like undulations, its almost imperceptible cradle-like swaying accompanying the soft rhythm of the trapeze and the double shadow of the man projected onto the top of the curtain by the two beams of electric light.

Leaning forward a little, the woman also grabs a trapeze with one hand and restrains herself by a rope held in the other. In the meantime, the man topples over, remaining suspended by his feet on the bar of his trapeze, motionless, upside down, his arms stretched out.

Then, the waltz stops dead. An ominous silence descends, broken suddenly by an explosion from a champagne bottle. A shiver runs through the audience, an 'All right!' resounds around the hall. The woman hurls herself through the air, flies beneath the light of the chandeliers, then, letting go of the trapeze, she falls, feet foremost, into the arms of the man, who to the shattering crash of a cymbal and to the increasingly triumphant and joyful reprise of the waltz swings her for a moment by the feet, then throws her into the net where, with her silver and azure-blue tights, she rebounds like a fish twisting and jumping in a cast-net.

The sound of stamping feet, clapping hands and canes being struck on the floorboards accompanies the acrobats' descent. As they disappear behind a piece of scenery, the shouting becomes even more tumultuous; the man and woman reappear, one bowing very low, the other blowing kisses with both hands, then, with a little, childish jump, they retire once again into the wings.

As the net is gathered up again, the hall is once more filled with the sound of breaking waves.

* * *

And then suddenly, I'm thinking of Antwerp, of the great port where, amid a similar rolling sound, you hear the 'All right!' of English sailors about to put to sea. And yet it's in this way that the most disparate places and things come together, through an analogy that seems bizarre at first sight. You evoke in the place you happen to be, the pleasures of the place you are not. This topsy-turvy fact cuts both ways. Like when a fleeting pleasure inspired by the present is diverted just as it's fading and coming to an end, and is renewed and prolonged in another which, seen through the eye of memory, becomes at one and the same time both sweeter and more real.

V

The ballet begins. The scenery vaguely suggests the inside of a seraglio, full of hooded women who waddle

about like she-bears. A fancy-dress Ottoman, head
wrapped in a turban and mouth furnished with a
chibouk, cracks his whip. The hoods fall away, revealing dancing girls, enlisted from the depths of some
suburb, who start to skip around to common dancehall music, enlivened from time to time by the tune
of 'Old Bugeaud's Cap', no doubt introduced into
this mazurka to justify the arrival of a bevy of
women dressed like spahis.

It's at this moment, under the streams of electric
light that flood the stage, that a whirlpool of white
tuile appears, spattered with blue fire and with naked
flesh writhing at the centre; then the *première dan-
seuse*, recognisable by her silk leggings, does a little
point work on her toes, shakes the false sequins that
surround her like a ring of golden dots, leaps up and
collapses into her skirts, simulating a fallen flower,
petals on the ground and stalk in the air.

But all this bank-holiday orientalism bursting like
a loud *grand finale* cannot distract the connoisseur,
who, out of all these great lumps of women rhythmically shaking themselves silly, is interested only in
one, the one dressed as a spahi officer, with her large,
billowing blue pantaloons, her dainty red boots, her
gold-braided spencer, and her little scarlet waistcoat,
skin-tight, moulding her breasts and showing off
their erect tips. She dances like a goat, but she is
adorable and common, with her braided kepi, her
wasp waist, her large backside, her retroussé nose,
and her look of a pleasantly roguish tom-boy. Such
as she is, this girl evokes images of barricades and
torn up streets, exhales a whiff of *trois-six* and

gunpowder, calls to mind the epic poem of an armed rabble, the bombast of civil war mixed with drunken debaucheries.

In front of her, you inevitably think of those over-excited periods in our history, of those uprisings in which Marianne of Belleville charges off to save a nation or to stave in a wine-barrel.

VI

A cemetery backdrop; to the right, a tombstone with this inscription: *Here lies . . . killed in a duel.* Night time; some muted music; nobody.

Suddenly, from behind scenery 'flats' on the left and right of the stage, two pierrots in black costumes advance slowly, followed by their seconds: the first, tall, thin, recalling the type created by Deburau, a long horse's head, flour-covered, eyes blinking beneath white lids; the other more thick-set, stockier, with a stub nose, his sarcastic, cadaverous face split by the red hole of his mouth.

The impression produced by the entrance of these men is chilling and noble. The comedy drawn from the juxtaposition of their black bodies and plaster faces disappears; this is no longer some sordid theat-rical illusion. Life itself rises up before us, breathless and magnificent.

The pierrots read the inscription on the tombstone and step back a pace; trembling, they turn their heads and see a doctor about to unroll some bandages and calmly arranging his medical bag.

The anguish of a face in the process of a break-down passes over their pale countenances; fear, that terrible nervous sickness, nails them quivering to the spot.

After being placed face to face, one opposite the other, the sight of epées being drawn from serge cloth covers scares them even more. The trembling of their hands increases, their legs wobble, their throats choke, their mouths work in silence, saliva-less tongues beat, searching for breath, their fingers wander and clutch at the cravats they should be untying.

Then their fear increases still more and becomes so imperious and so terrible, that their already rebellious nerves suddenly break down and they go to pieces, no one can hold them. A single idea surges up in their disordered minds, to take flight, and they rush off, knocking over everything; but they are pursued and brought back by the seconds who place them face to face again, epées in hand.

Then, after one final revolt of the flesh which rises up against the carnage awaiting it, the energy of cornered beasts comes to them and they throw themselves, madly, one onto the other, striking and stabbing at random, roused by incredible leaps, unconscious, blinded and deafened by the flashing and chinking of steel, and then suddenly falling, exhausted, like puppets whose strings have broken.

Finishing in a lavish farce, in a disorganised charge, this cruel study of the human machine in the grip of fear has convulsed the hall with guffaws. From a close study of this laughter, it seems to me that the public saw nothing in this admirable pantomime but a parade of grotesques, intended, no doubt, to complete the appearance of a fairground which the Folies-Bergère assumes in those corners in which it sets up gambling wheels, games of *boule*, bearded women and shooting galleries.

For more reflective and more alert minds, though, it's another matter. The whole aesthetics of the English school of caricature is once again brought into play in the scenarios of these side-splitting, yet funereal clowns, the Hanlon-Lees. Their pantomime, so true in its frigid mania, so ferociously comical in its exaggeration, is nothing less than a new and charming incarnation of that lugubrious farce, that sinister buffoonery so unique to that splenetic country, and which has previously been expressed and condensed by those marvellous and forceful artists, Hogarth and Rowlandson, Gillray and Cruickshank.

VII

As far as the Folies is concerned, there are two indispensable and delightful types of waltz: one twirling and joyous, expressing the poise of the trapeze, the amazing somersaults of the acrobats, the rhythm of a body that raises and lowers itself by the strength of its own arms, sways, held only by its legs, then up again, head brushing past stomach and abdomen, the arms taking the place of feet which beat the air with their chalk-dusted shoes; the other morbidly voluptuous, displaying the bloodshot eyes and trembling hands of those caught *in flagrante delicto*, of passions stalled by the presence of a third, of debaucheries aborted in full flow for lack of stamina, of bodies contorted and expectant, ending at last with the triumphant crash of cymbals and brasses in the cry of pain and joy of the climax.

It would be meaningless to play, say, *Robert le Diable* in this hall. It would jar like the face of a respectable old man engaged in an illicit *tête-à-tête*. Here, one must have rotten, uncouth music, something that envelopes with vulgar caresses, with street kisses, with twenty-franc assignations, the chatter of those who have dined copiously and expensively, people tired of stewing over their murky business affairs, dragging into this theatre promenade their worries about scams that might turn out badly, uneasy about their dubious dealings in shares and in women, but cheered by the high spirits of fraudsters whose tricks have come off and who get tipsy with painted women to the sound of loutish music.

VIII

What is truly admirable, truly unique, is that this theatre has a real air of the boulevards about it.

It is ugly and it is superb, it is in both exquisitely good and outrageously bad taste. It's also unfinished, like anything that aims to be truly beautiful. The *faux jardin*, with its raised walkways, its arcades of rough wooden latticework with solid lozenges and cut-out trefoils stained red ochre and gold, its canopy of pompommed and tasselled material, striped

garnet-red and greyish-brown, its fake Louvois fountains with three women back-to-back sandwiched
between two enormous saucers of imitation bronze
set amid green tufts, its pathways carpeted with
tables, rattan divans and chairs, with bars tended by
amply made-up women, resembles at one and the
same time the restaurant on the Rue Montesquieu
and a Turkish or Algerian bazaar.

Alhambresque *à la* Poyet, Moorish *à la* Duval,
with, what's more, the vague smell of those bar-
saloons in the old suburbs decorated with oriental
columns and mirrors, this theatre, with its auditorium whose faded reds and tarnished golds clash
with the brand-new luxury of the *faux jardin*, is the
only place in Paris that stinks so deliciously of the
make-up of bought caresses and the desperation of
depravities that fail to excite.

II. DANCE NIGHT AT THE *BRASSERIE EUROPÉENNE* IN GRENELLE

I settled myself at a café table next to two ladies who were deep in conversation. One, a jolly, red-faced woman with bright eyes and grey hair, was adjusting the bow of a carob-brown scarf with her stubby hand; the other, jaundiced and slightly drawn, was obstinately taking snuff from an old horn snuff-box.

Every time they spoke, these ladies referred to each other by name; the red-faced one addressed her neighbour as Madame Haumont, and she in her turn was called Madame Tampois.

From where I was sitting, on a small platform reached by two steps, I overlooked the dance-floor.

A little above me, to the right, rose the tiers of the orchestra; to the left, overhanging a pool of stagnant water, rose the rocks of a fake grotto where three pink plaster statues stood in their carved togas against a wall on which a Swiss valley scene was painted. The dancehall of the *Brasserie Européenne* was divided by a balustrade into two sections: the first, forming a large lobby buttressed by cast-iron columns and floored with asphalt, was furnished with tables and chairs and canopied with drapes that had once been green but were now rotting from the gas flames and dripping water; the second, stretching out like a great hall, was similarly supported by pillars and topped by a ridged glass roof. You might as well

have been in a provincial railway station as in this
hall, with its cracked and faded walls, and the resem-
blance was accentuated still further by the dismal
lighting, similar to that of a station waiting-room, by
the three red and green lamps that were flaring
through the smoke at the back of the hall like signal
lights, and by an immense glass partition separating
the dancehall from the brasserie itself, a partition
that glimmered in the gaslight amid billows of steam
and gave the impression of a poorly-lit railway line
receding, in the mists of the night, into the distance.

On this suburban station platform, an enormous
crowd was seething and, under the strident whistles
of flutes, under the continuous banging of a big
drum, quartermasters, administrative clerks, medical orderlies, staff clerks and recruitment clerks, a
whole army of white-fringed epaulettes were march-
ing around, tossing blue arms into the air and fling-
ing red legs onto the floorboards; some, heads bald,
craniums shaved and dripping with sweat, were simulating the opening and closing of scissor-blades with
their legs; others, kepis squashed against their necks,
were swaying their hips, holding up the tails of their
coats between two fingers, like dancing-girls pinching
their skirts; others still, hands on their bellies,
seemed to be grinding coffee or turning a starting
handle, while a medical orderly, attempting a *cavalier
seul*, leaped about, his tibias twisting like jacket
sleeves, his contorted arms and clenched fists seem-
ing to want to uncork the parquet floor like a bottle.

The women were, for the most part, less frenetic,
more composed. Almost all were decorously skipping

around, showing off with affected twirls, having put on at the same time as their party frocks a Sunday-best dignity that was maintained by the presence of relatives seated on the wooden benches against the wall.

Some of them, well turned out and decked with pretentious trinkets, had preserved the former elegance of the tobacco-girls of the Gros-Caillou *quartier* to which they belonged; they flaunted long, eight-button gloves, bought for fifteen sous at the dry-cleaner's, and two of them, squeezed into matt black Indian cashmir dresses with jade necklaces that rained sparkling drops around their necks, were shrewishly strutting about on the arms of two butchers from the Grenelle abattoir, strapping fellows with complexions the colour of raw meat, and garish scarves tied in sailor-knots over their long-sleeved, knitted waistcoats.

These latter had neither the precise gestures, nor the affected bearing of the military men. More common, though less vulgar, they were heaving their copious bellies as they danced, puffing out their cheeks, play-acting at being breathless and, like cabbies in cold weather, clumsily jumping up and down, feet together as if tied, and throwing their arms around their shoulders.

– Look, there's Ninie! Hey, Ninie!

This cry cut across the blasts of the orchestra; a gap opened up in the middle of a group of infantry-men, out of which shot a little plump girl who flung herself right into the middle of the quadrille, and, skirts up to her belly, kicked her legs, showing off under the white calico of her knickerbockers the bare flesh of her thighs.

— Ow! watch it, Titine, she shouted to her opposite number, a snotty-nosed girl of sixteen, her jutting mouth revealing beneath a snub nose some tiny, gappy teeth, stunted as if filed down, who, in the middle of the circle of dancers, was repeatedly hoisting into the air a thin leg, made thinner still by bright red lisle stockings.

— She really is quite disgustingly abandoned when she dances, said Madame Tampois, pointing out Ninie, who, hands on hips fishwife-fashion, was now jiggling her breasts, rolling her eyes blankly to the ceiling, and rapidly flicking the pointed tip of her tongue in and out of her mouth.

— And that little brat with her stockings, look at her, replied Madame Haumont folding her arms. At her age, would you believe it! No, really, two monstrosities like that, it's enough to stop respectable people bringing their daughters to the dance.

The two old ladies drank a mouthful of beer, then once again tried to restore balance to the heap of cloaks and hats on a nearby chair.

— Look, there are so many people here.

— Oh, don't talk to me about it, I'm suffocating!

— And business, Madame Tampois, is it going well?

— Very slowly, Madame Haumont, as you know, you don't get rich quick in the haberdashery business.

— Ah, now what the devil's become of Léonie, sighed Madame Haumont, can you see her anywhere? But Madame Tampois made a sign that she couldn't hear her. The quadrille was nearing its end, and as if overtaken by madness, the clarinets were blowing fit to burst, the brass lashed the hall with a hail of sound, while the bass drum boomed amid a crash of broken glass from furiously shaken cymbals.

At last the musicians came to a stop, exhausted; some wiped their foreheads and their necks; others, out of breath, emptied the saliva trapped in their trombones; cymbals, yellow and spotted with black patches like huge crêpes, lay next to drumsticks on the top of a drum.

– Here they are, and about time too! said Madame Haumont catching sight of her daughter, who was making her way over towards her on the arm of a staff sergeant. Go on Léonie, wrap yourself up warm, and she threw a cloak over her shoulders. Come on, drink a little, and she offered her a glass of lukewarm wine which she'd ordered during the dance. But her daughter protested, she was thirsty and wanted to drink something cold.

– When you're in a sweat, you drink something hot, said her mother, wiping her daughter's forehead and raising the glass to her lips.

– What about you, Jules, said Madame Tampois, do you want to drink this beer?

– Well, Auntie, replied the sergeant, I won't say no because it's a bit on the hot side. He smacked his lips. Really, it does you good whichever way it goes down, he continued, wiping his moustache. Hello, there's Cabannes, hey! over here old chap, how're you doing?

– Not so bad, announced Cabannes in his nasal voice, a medical orderly sergeant with a freckled face

51

and carroty hair; politely, he bowed to the ladies and after a moment's silence, he added:

— Gives you a thirst, here.

No one seemed to take any notice of the new-comer's observation.

— Can I get anyone anything? shouted a waiter rushing up.

No one breathed a word.

— Nothing, said Madame Tampois finally.

— You get served quicker that way, said Cabannes, in a melancholy tone tinged with sarcasm.

— Quite so, Auguste, replied the good lady calmly; she took out her snuffbox, offered it to Madame Haumont and then placed a pinch of snuff on the palm of her hand which she inhaled deeply, with a sniff of her nose.

A polka began, shaking the windows which trembled as if a lorry-load of sheet metal was passing by. Jules offered his arm to Léonie. Cabannes cast a glance around the table at the two old women, turned on his heels and, without bowing, he too disappeared into the tide of dancers.

— There's no way to make yourself heard above this blessed music, groaned Madame Tampois. Explosions of brass were bursting in her ears; she turned round and stared furiously at an old trombonist with a huge bespectacled nose and distended cheeks which glowed like a monkey's bare backside, who was pulling and pushing his brass slide in and out with great heaves of his stomach.

— Absolutely unbelievable! Eh, don't you think, my dear? but her friend was no longer listening; her eyes were following her daughter off in the distance, through the crowd. She could only see the girl's back, her face being pressed against that of the sergeant's; by turns, the red of his trousers and the white of his epaulettes, then the black of her dress and the white of her petticoats, appeared and disappeared in a whirl. Soon she lost Léonie completely from view; a reddish dust was rising from the floorboards and, mixing with the steamy, bath-house atmosphere, hung in suspension under the roof. Below her, here and there in the swarming crowd, innumerable red breeches were doing the galop and dark-blue coat-tails, speckled with the silver and gold dots of their buttons, were flapping around above them; on all sides, next to girl's faces, epaulette fringes were crawling like maggots.

The dancehall seemed to be quivering; the signal lights were slowly winking in the mist; silhouettes of soldiers and girls were moving around now like blurs, as if in hot, cloudy water.

Water-drops were falling from the ceiling where the steam was starting to condense; Madame Haumont raised her nose in the air.

– Can you understand why they left the roof on? Ah! Thérésa, how are you? and she interrupted her line of thought to shake hands with a tall, beautiful girl who was coming up the steps followed by a cuirassier.

A faded beauty, but still pretty beneath her layers of pink face-powder and her hair cut in a tooth-comb fringe, she strutted about in a hooped dress of soot-black Pekin silk striped with satin and faille, underneath which sparkled a petticoat of gathered blue satin lined with cream lace. A glimpse of peacock-blue stockings and reddish-brown ankle-boots could be seen when she leaned back a little to lift off an immense d'Artagnan hat, in garnet-red plush, that was pinned on the left with a grey dove broach.

– And is everything still going as well you'd like? she said sitting down, showing off fingers loaded with rings and adorned with polished nails, artificial pink in colour and shaped like spoons.

– You, she said brusquely to the cuirassier, what would you like, wine or beer?

– Wine!

– Waiter, a bottle of wine! Then, without taking any more notice of the cuirassier, she continued:

– And what about Léonie and her cough?

– There's little change; it's no use telling yourself it's nothing, you worry about it just the same; and what's more, she's not very sensible, she likes to dance too much . . . anyway, you'll see her soon yourself, she's over there.

Thérésa cast a sidelong glance at the enormous soldier who was drinking in silence next to her; his bull-neck supported a lumbering, close-cropped skull, a low forehead, and a thick yellow moustache. In the blink of an eye, she seemed to weigh up the strength of his shoulders, the power of his thighs and loins, the promise of his wild, brutish bearing, then she got up and, eyes fixed on the promenade encircling the dancefloor, she appeared to size up the build and the bestial features of the other cuirassiers filling the tables; she smiled, satisfied, fell back into her chair, and ordered another bottle.

— Thérésa, said Madame Haumont, gently pulling her by the sleeve, there's Léonie.

— Well! what a good-for-nothing creature that woman is, whispered Madame Tampois. She doesn't even know that soldier . . .

But Madame Haumont replied stiffly:

— She's the daughter of old Gillet . . . you know, the man who's lived for years on the same floor as us, an engineer at Cail et Cie. Thérésa may enjoy a good time, that's her lookout, but you mark my words, that woman has no equal as far as honesty is concerned; she wouldn't cheat anyone out of a *sous*. And besides, she lives in a very luxurious place you know, if only you could see it . . . what's more, she's being kept by a respectable gentleman . . .

And in a confidential tone she added:

— A member of the nobility, my dear.

— Is that so, said Madame Tampois and she contemplated Thérésa with respect. She has got what one might call a distinguished face, she said, loud enough to be overheard. Thérésa smiled and, encouraged, Madame Tampois readied herself to sidle into the conversation between Thérésa and Léonie, who were each trying to out-talk the other, when her nephew the sergeant caught her attention. Below her, on the dance floor, he was imploring her with his eyes and imitating the gesture of a man emptying a glass with his hand.

— No, no, said the old woman, you can do well enough without your tipple for one night. Have you ever seen anything like it!

Jules didn't insist; he trotted off and rejoined a

group of his comrades who, during the orchestra interval, were walking around the enclosure reserved for dancing. They were strutting about, hands in pockets which they flared out as they lolled, shouting with laughter, impeding women, indulging in frantic races with tobacconists' assistants and young laundry-girls, chasing each other like little kids, shouting loudly amid the dust raised by their gallivanting, and falling over to amuse their cronies. Scattered among the soldiers, the contemptuous civilians remained calm: aside from a few pimps who had slipped out from dives such as the Salon de Mars and the Ardoise, a few drapers' assistants, and a few skilled workers dressed in suits like them but distinguishable by their worn nails and their blackened fingers; aside from a few butchers from Grenelle, a few tobacconists, and a few clerks from the Ministry, mostly belonging to the War Office, it was men of the Commissariat who dominated the hall, adjusting the points of their wilting moustaches, striking various poses, and staring at the spectators with a resolute air, as befits men adored by the whole adolescent female population of Gros-Caillou and Grenelle, as befits the absolute masters of a conquered country.

However, next to the lively, noisy party of infantrymen overspreading the area in front of the orchestra under the glass ceiling, another quieter, more sombre group was establishing itself under the canvas-roofed promenade. Here, detachments of dragoons, artillerymen and soldiers from the service corps, entire squadrons of cuirassiers were drinking. Their bulky uniforms and the express injunction against dancing in the ballroom area with spurs on, even when covered, prevented them from joining in the polkas and the quadrilles. They were looking around at the infantrymen and the tobacco-girls in disdain, despising these foot-sloggers and their little girls who didn't appreciate their tall physiques, waiting for more experienced women, more lavish in money and in vice who, at midnight, came back over from the other side of the river in order to rediscover the dissolute pleasures of their native *quartier*.

– I'm going to dance, shouted Thérésa, getting up. You've still got some wine left, drink up, she said, addressing the cuirassier who was quietly smoking, and she leapt off the platform and plunged into the infantrymen.

– Oh, just my luck! she said, coming to a stop in front of a man dressed in a filthy, nut-brown coat, dirty tweed trousers, clapped-out patent-leather boots with worn heels, and a blackcurrant-coloured scarf around his greasy collar that hid his shirt.

But an immense clamour drowned her voice. A cry of 'a waltz, a waltz!' was taken up by the whole hall.

– Stay here, dear, said Madame Haumont to Léonie. You're tired and it's late.

– Oh, just one turn, she said, seeing Jules approaching her, and, led off by the sergeant, she disappeared into the smoke.

– It's almost midnight, sighed her mother, annoyed, and today's Sunday so it's late-night dancing. I really wanted to leave before all the whores arrived. There, Madame Tampois, just as I'm telling you, here they come!

And, indeed, through the wide-open doors gushed a noisy confusion of hats and petticoats; beneath thickets of plumes and tail-feathers, beneath felt musketeer hats with extravagant brims, ovals of pink face-powder were being tossed back, split by scarlet-rimmed holes from which raucous yells escaped. They were immediately answered by wild hurrahs and the sound of boots loudly reverberating across the dancefloor. Squadrons of cavalry spurred themselves into action, charging, arms open in front of them, at the whores. It was a riot of uniforms and skirts, a mass of red, black and white, a whirlpool of bodies in which naked arms could be seen entwined around the necks of cuirassiers, the shaven napes of whom still predominated over the plumes and feathers. The corridor into which the cavalrymen were crowding disappeared under a dust cloud, from which came a rumbling like an engine overheating; then the trembling of the dancehall ceased, smothered by the hurricane of a quadrille.

— It's so smoky, you can't see anything, said Madame Tampois, tomorrow, for sure, my handkerchief will be black.

— And what a racket! said Madame Haumont stuffing her fingers in her ears.

Taking no notice of the cavalrymen's charges, the regiments of the Commissariat unleashed an assault in their turn, carrying off tobacco girls by their waists. To one side, Ninie was pinning up a gaping hole in her drawers and large patches of sweat were spreading under her armpits almost as far as her breasts. To the pungent smell of horse-dung and rancid grease emanating from the agitated uniforms of the cavalrymen, was now added the pestilential aroma of warm riding-boots and hot hob-nailed shoes, the fetid perfume of unwashed armpits and cheap make-up.

– The hussy, sighed Madame Haumont, looking round for her daughter. Ah, you've decided to come back, and not a moment too soon. Come on now, since you're here let's hurry up, it's getting late. While the women put their coats on, the ineffectual sergeant kissed his aunt and briskly shook everyone's hand in turn; then they descended the dais and attempted to slip through the camp of cuirassiers. But at the first step, they had to stop.

– Let's go back the way we came to the dancehall, suggested Madame Tampois. Follow me, Léonie, I'm holding the hand-rail. And she skirted the balustrade separating the two sections of the hall, but their retreat was now barred on this side, too: they could no longer go either forwards or backwards. A small gap opened up, into which Madame Tampois threw herself; Madame Haumont and her daughter plunged in behind her, but they were immediately brought up short, banging their noses against her back; the haberdasher's body completely filled the opening she had entered; Madame Tampois was gripped as if between two doors. Furious, she heaved her whole weight against the people who surrounded her; by poking her elbows, she cleared a way through the crowd, sweeping Léonie, who was pushing her mother along with her, while I followed up the rear. And amid the jeers of jostled women, amid the swearing of waiters whose trays of beer wobbled above their heads, amid cannibal cries yelled by the troops, they finally reached the door of the brasserie.

– Do your cloak up properly, my girl, said Madame Haumont, but the café was overflowing with soldiers, and none of the exits were free.

Here, cavalrymen and infantrymen were drinking pell-mell, *en masse*; the two distinct milieux of the dancehall were mixing together in this immense hall, full of billiard-tables and benches. Heaps of saucers and glasses were piling up on the tables. On all sides, there were coat-stands and hat pegs on which glittered the accessories of war: cuirassiers' helmets with black horse-hair manes or purple plumes, trumpeters' helmets with their vermillion tails, shakos with copper stars under their cockades, madder-red kepis, cartridge pouches, sabre-bayonets, long cavalry swords whose shining brass hilts and steel scabbards were hanging everywhere above the seats. And in the breeze from the opening doors, weapons tinkled, horse-hair manes quivered and slow ripples ran along helmet crests and ruffled their plumes.

A continuous hubbub was rising amid steam from onion soup and sauerkraut; every now and again, the staccato whistle of flutes could be heard in the café as well as the distant rumble of a bass drum.

– Hey, Léonie!

The three women turned round; in an alcove, a young girl, dressed head to foot in crushed black velvet, the lobes of her ears glowing like two points of fire, was seated opposite a medical orderly.

– Well, well, it's Louise, said Léonie, kissing her on both cheeks.

– And how are you, Madame Tampois?

– Very well.

– You've just come from the ball?

– But of course.

– Let me kiss you, Madame Haumont. Look, there's plenty of room here, sit yourselves down.

– Damn, but they're a fine couple of lookers, murmured the medical orderly.

– I say you, try not to be so ill-mannered at least, said Madame Tampois.

– Look Casimir, just shut up, ordered Louise.

– No, my dear, no, it's too late. We're going to bed, said Madame Haumont, declining the chair that had been offered her.

But the young girl insisted.

– If you stay standing like that in a draught, between the door into the dancehall and the door out onto the road, Léonie will catch cold. Come on, Madame Haumont, sit down and have a drink.

– So be it, replied the old lady. Only Léonie will drink something as a tonic, some hot wine perhaps.

– Oh, no! cried Léonie. I've had enough of your hot wine, I want to drink some beer.

They immediately fell to quarrelling.

– Why couldn't Mademoiselle drink both? suggested the medical orderly.

With a look that cut him down to size, Madame Haumont taught the soldier not to interfere in her affairs. A waiter passed by.

– A beer! said Léonie.

61

Madame Haumont shook her head.

– Oh, these young people, she sighed.

Then turning to Louise she said:

– Well, Louise, what about the tobacco business, anything new?

– The same old thing, Madame Haumont, always the same thing, nothing changes. You slave away from morning to night, and you get paid next to nothing.

– The fact is, replied the old lady inspecting the young girl's apparel, the fact is that if government money had to pay for velvet like that . . . and, full of envy, she felt the material between her thumb and index finger.

– You said it, said Louise laughing. Oh, you'd certainly need to roll a lot of cigarettes!

– Now what about Berthe, how is she doing?

– Why, not too bad.

– Is she still hand-rolling cigarettes?

– Oh no, didn't you know, she works on the cigarette machine now.

– Never! – By the way, you know that Thérésa is here at the dance?

– Look, there he is again, interrupted Madame Tampois pointing to Sergeant Cabannes who was prowling around the table. Go on, clear off you idler, 'If you're hungry eat your fist, if you're thirsty . . .'

But she couldn't remember the rest of the phrase.

– Children, she said, changing the conversation and taking a pinch of snuff, it's stifling in here.

– For sure, said Louise to no one in particular, distracted by the ostentatious outfits of two whores with sunken eyes, their matchstick-black lashes fluttering over two patches of rouge plastered on their cheeks, their elegant but creased dresses fastened by bits of ribbon and heavy-duty safety pins, two whores obviously from brothels on the other side of the river. They were making, between the two of them, a terrible racket; they had asked for a bottle of beer and the waiter, confused by all the orders, had placed a bottle, right there in front of them without opening it. So now they were bawling to attract his attention, while he, far off in the distance, was shouting 'Coming!' and carrying trays of beer to the other end of the hall.

— Coming my arse! said one of them. She resolutely gripped the neck of the bottle and tried to remove the cork with her teeth, but she pulled in vain, her features contorting under the greasepaint on her face.

— It's no good, she said, wiping her lipstick-less lips with her handkerchief and replacing the bottle, its cork now stained pink.

All around them now the tables were loaded with food and drink, and the chairs full of soldiers and women.

Here, a whore, straddled across the knees of a cavalryman, was furiously clasping his legs between her thighs and rubbing, almost ecstatically, her thin stockings against his leggings; there, another was having her fingers crushed by the large paw of a cuirassier who was squeezing her rings together, and she was crying and almost swooning with pain and desire. Two rows of tables further off, a tall woman, wearing a marvellous plum-coloured satin bolero topped by a large bouquet of yellow feathers, was calmly eating onion soup next to a drunken artilleryman dribbling saliva between his two boots, holding her spoon up high in order to catch the strands of cheese and then suck them in. Alone, abandoned no doubt, a young girl was staring fixedly in front of her and wistfully chewing the end of a matchstick.

A billiard ball, clumsily struck by a medical orderly, leaped off a billiard table and rolled under a bench; the scraping of disturbed chairs, the stamping of feet, and the ridiculous exclamations of women echoed round the room. A soldier who had been sick and then brought round by his friends had collapsed on a bench, his face distorted, stinking of sour wine and ammonia; nearby, a drunken whore was asleep in front of her plate of sauerkraut, which a quartermaster was surreptitiously picking at.

Soon, amid the drunkenness of this wild parade-ground party, the arguments began. The soldier's passion for regimental loyalty, his querulous instincts, his lust for savagery and his enthusiasm for battle were starting to awake; disputes would begin first at one table, then spread to all the others. Already, a cuirassier, standing with his back towards me, his arms restrained by more sober friends, was insulting a seated soldier I couldn't see, while behind a billiard table, two Grenelle pimps with drawling voices were threatening to knife one another as soon as they left the dancehall.

— It's getting sordid. Come on, let's go while the road's clear, ordered Madame Haumont.

It certainly was getting sordid, and I'd inhaled enough of the stench and bodily sweat of the military to passionately desire a cordial breath of pure, still air. I did as those sturdy women whose words and gestures I had so scrupulously spied on had done: I left.

Once out on the Avenue de Lowendal in the middle of the night, in the solitude of that dead *quartier*, I took stock of the facts I had just acquired; they seemed to me to unite and blend themselves into this axiom: in Gros-Caillou and Grenelle, love begins, for very young girls, with staff clerks and quartermasters, and ends, for very mature women, with the toughest cavalrymen and soldiers of the service corps.

Then, all too often, in the expectation of having their absinthes paid for by the former earnings of these old streetwalkers, retired captains from all services take up these imitation Magdalens and marry them, at the very point when their maturity has become such that, despite the certainty of their pension, even the heavy cavalry take fright!

III. PARISIAN CHARACTERS

THE BUS CONDUCTOR

– Stop, stop!
  – Ding!
  – Ouf!

And with skirts gathered-up and her face as red as a peony, the stout old woman, gripped under the arm by the conductor, stumbles into the bus and flops herself down with a dull grunt between the two little mahogany rails that mark out her place.

The conductor digs in his satchel and hands some change to the huge lump of a woman spilling out of her seat, then he climbs to the top of the bus where, crammed on wooden benches, men's bodies are being painfully tossed around behind the back of the driver as he cracks his whip. Leaning on the rail of the top deck, he collects his three *sous* and then goes down again, seating himself on a small fold-out seat which blocks the entrance to the bus. Nothing more to do. It's then that our man looks casually at the unfortunates who are rolling along, jolted amid the noise of clanking iron, shaking windows, horses' farts and the clanging of the bell. He listens to the whining of a little brat seated on his mother's knees, whose legs are beating rhythmically on neighbouring knee-caps;

then, tired of looking at these two rows of passengers nodding to each other at every bump, he turns aside and vaguely contemplates the street.

What can he be thinking about as the carriage runs lopsidedly along, always through the same gutters, always along the same streets? To distract him there are placards that sway in the wind advertising apartments to let, shops closed because of a death or a wedding, and the litter rotting in the doorway of a rich invalid. All that's very fine in the morning, when this bucket-on-wheels begins its Danaide-like task of picking up and throwing out, turn and turn about its flood of passengers, but for the rest of the day, after he's spelled out the posters and annoyed the greengrocer's dog who yaps as soon as he sees him, what is there to do, what is there to think about? Life would be intolerably monotonous if, from time to time, he didn't catch the odd pickpocket, hand in a pocket that wasn't his own. And this gathering of men and women, doesn't it provide him with a spectacle as old as the world, but one that's nevertheless eternally amusing? A young lady sits with her eyes closed, a young man opposite her. By what stratagem do these two beings, who have never seen each other before, come, without saying a word and by common accord, to get off one after the other and go round the same street corner? Ah, in default of voice or gesture, what passionate or romantic phrases can be expressed by a leg that furtively draws near, rubs against its neighbour like an amorous cat caressing and purring, draws back a little, sensing the other trying to get out of its clutches, then returns again and, finding the resistance less determined, risks a soft squeeze of the foot!

What memories of youth, eh, conductor? Do you recall those early years before a well-dressed man with a sash around his belly had you united by indissoluble ties, in the name of the law, to the torment of your life, to your cursed Melanie! Ah, you've time enough now to think about that country girl who knocks you about, who makes you eat cold dinners, and who treats you as a good-for-nothing idler if you've drunk a few more glasses of that sublime local wine than usual.

If only he had the means to divorce her and take another, to be like Machut who is so happy in his domestic set-up, life would be easier, the brats would be better brought up and better fed, and he could endure the reproaches of his boss with a little more patience. And so the disappointed husband gazes at a milliner's assistant at the other end of the bus who is staring through the window, past the horses' galloping rumps, at the teeming streets. She has a gentle air, this little one, her hands still pink . . . one could be happy with someone so young . . . yes, but—

– Passengers for Courcelles!

– Do you have to change?

– Numbers 8, 9, 10, get on.

– Ding! ding! ding!

And the bus goes off again with its cargo of arms, heads and legs. The young girl has got off and trots off into the distance with her oilcloth bag. The conductor can't help thinking about her and he passes in review all the qualities she might have had.

71

He imagines seeing her blush at the soft prickle of his moustache; ah, she certainly wouldn't be like his crotchety and cantankerous wife. He's a hundred miles from reality and living completely in the land of dreams when the familiar cry recalls him once more to the exigencies of work.

– Stop! Stop!

– Ding!

THE STREETWALKER

For her, as for the others, vice has performed its customary task. It has refined and made desirable the brazen ugliness of her face. Losing none of the suburban grace of her origins, the whore has become, with her gaudy finery and her charms audaciously worked up with powders and pastes, a tempting aperitif for those jaded palates, those flagging appetites, aroused only by exuberant make-up and the tumult of over-theatrical frocks.

She has attained to that distinction among the rabble, so delightful in whores from the lower classes. The slut has lost the weather-beaten complexion and stale smell so typical of filthy poverty; now, the ash of Cuban *Conchas* cigars replaces pipe-dottle, the wine glass replaces the mug, bottles of the finest vintage, velvety with dust, the crude litre-bottles of *picolo* and *vin ordinaire*, the iron bunk is swapped for a large bed, upholstered with fabrics and canopied with mirrors; now, the streetwalker dazzles with her façade of flesh carefully touched up with bichloride of mercury and powder. Then suddenly one evening, comes the downfall. Polyte, who has secretly been dishing her up a love sullied by kicks from his boot, rashly stays beyond his time and her earnest,

Jean-Louis Forain's *L'Ambulante* (*The Streetwalker*, left) was originally intended to illustrate the story of the same name, but was excluded from the published edition, perhaps because it didn't reflect the story's downbeat nature. It was substituted by *Le Noeud de Cravate* (*Knotting a tie*, right), which refers to an incident in the story itself.

benevolent bank clerk gives her up and returns to his family, where he reproaches his sons daily about the laxity of their morals.

Good times give way to bad as a garrison of men of all ages billet themselves on her; on the watch in front of a café, her dark-ringed eyes set snares, but the sad, impudent smile on her mouth scares off the average John, who desires only the bliss of non-descript kisses and the usual predictable charade.

From now on, her mysterious and sinister beauty remains unappreciated and, in the heat, in the cold, for whole evenings, for whole nights, she remains on the look-out, poaching, firing on game that scurries off, or, on her lucky nights, bringing down the odd drunkard.

But for the most part, she returns home empty-handed, starving, her stomach's hunger assuaged by drink, her lungs racked with phlegm, and she goes to bed, overwhelmed, alone, thinking of the terrible lout who has ruined her, of their eager assignations in the wine-shop on the Place Pinel whose wretched façade is adorned with these words: 'Drink Rigolboche'.

However distant and blurred those times may be, the streetwalker still dreams of them in those fits of lucid insomnia induced by endless drinking bouts and fatigue. Drained and exhausted, she still flinches at the memory of the caresses and the free drinks she heaped on that man. The details of her touching and stupid fascination come back to her; she sees again his hair curled over his ears like bull's horns, his pea-green shirts, his ties which she knotted for him herself, his little kisses and his wheedling when he wanted money to buy his other conquests a glass of Rigolboche, that rose-tinted, vanilla-flavoured essence, that liqueur of rag-and-bone men!

And the morning light floods her bedroom, and the afternoon passes; she has to get up and yoke herself yet again to the hard life that has been made for her. As it did yesterday, the day slips by, as it will again tomorrow. The number of buyers diminishes still further or else they cheat her meanly out of the price of her pains.

Swindled by day, swindled by night, consumed by an inextinguishable thirst, she can do nothing but quench Polyte's, who, as recompense, unleashes on her a prodigious hail of kicks with his boot.

Then this unrelenting decline gathers pace as these love-affairs and these beatings, these famines and these dissipations hollow out eyes that have now sunk deep into her bruised face. On pain of dying of hunger altogether, she must now pad out her wasted shoulderblades, and contain within the bounds of her corset the sagging flabbiness of her flesh; wadding, whalebones, face paint and pots of rouge are bleeding the streetwalker's funds dry. The harvest of her sins is ripe and the vice-squad threatens. Now, heave! onto the tip-cart, and off to the garrets of the Lourcine hospital with her!

THE WASHERWOMAN

Not since Nausicaa of Homeric and tedious memory have queens washed their own clothes themselves, and if I leave aside those 'goddesses' elected during *mi-carême*, amid the sloshing of pints and the bumping of glasses, the cleaning of petticoats and stockings has long since been consigned to scrubbers, whose stout arms make light work of ironing. Washerwomen no longer smell of benjamin and amber, as they did years ago, like Lancret's pink laundresses, and, if they exist today at all, they only occasionally exercise their trade, their true profession being no doubt more lucrative, if less mentionable.

Oh yes, they have a bad reputation . . . Oh yes, the old ones prowl around like bitches, scoffing and drinking, raging with thirst from the heat of the stoves . . . Oh yes, the young ones flirt, mad for love, and have a right old time on leaving the washhouse! And what of it? Do you think their lives are easy and that they haven't the right to bury the dreariness of a long day in the bottom of a winebottle or a bed? Oh, how they love and how they drink! Because to work standing up, under a rain constantly falling from washing hanging on lines, to feel water creep over the hairs of your neck and run slowly down the middle of your back, to breathe steam from the laundry in big gulps, to have your loins burnt by the fire of the furnace, to carry cartloads of sheets over your shoulder, to stagger under the weight of an enormous basket, to walk, to run, never to rest, to soak shirts in blue water, wring them, spin them, pass them over a hot fire and starch their cuffs, to goffer delicate linen or lose it altogether, to make holes in it, to have it sent back again by women who won't pay the bill and to get it accepted and paid for by men, such is their terrible job, their terrible life!

And yet how many of them will pass on to the final stages of this Passion play; their Stations of the Cross begins with the fanning of the stove and ends with the wash-tubs by the river! After old age has extinguished the desires of the flesh and raised up before them, like a supreme consolation, a glass of rot-gut; after wandering fruitlessly around the Rue aux Ours market until nine o'clock in the morning in search of a patroness desperate to have some laundry done, they run aground, catarrahal, in that *quartier* drenched by the sickly, snuff and medlar-coloured waters of the river Bièvre. Squatting there from the first blush of dawn till the last mists of evening, next to monstrosities dressed in rags, topped with head-scarves and buried up to their armpits in barrels, they soap for all they're worth, pummelling the laundry draining on boards with their battledores.

Seen from behind, when they are deep in a broth of dirty water, their spines protruding under their dirty *canezous*, twig-like strands of hair straggle in confusion over necks glazed like the skins of onions. And there they are, emaciated and sullen, sheltering their foam-specked heads under old red umbrellas, baying like wolves at the brats who insult them, straightening up their frames bent under packs of laundry, one fist on their hip, the other at the mouth by way of a megaphone, bawling at all those who pass those gobfuls of abuse that have earned them the slang nickname 'impudent tubs'.

THE JOURNEYMAN BAKER

Watteau! – melancholy inventor of black eyes that burn without fire and lips that are both provoking and frigid, painter of defenceless Cydalises whose pink silk trains are mirrored in lakes of blue – on one of these recent cold nights I was put in mind of your sardonic Gilles, his white face lit by anxious pupils and pierced by a round mouth like a red 'O' in a milky oval of flesh.

Strolling along a street on the outskirts of the city when the grills of tripe-butcher's shops, bathed in moonlight, throw their broken shadows across muddy streets, I glimpsed an inordinately tall marionette scurrying along the shopfronts, a bottle of wine in one hand, a pipe in the other.

I never doubted for a moment that this strange character was that playful and cunning trickster, that great uncorker of girls and deflowerer of bottles, the eternal rival of Harlequin: Pierrot. He was hugging the walls and had a sharp, cagey look about him. Suddenly, he halted in front of a house, pushed on a small door, fell into a black hole like a lily plunged up to its stalk in a bucket of ink, then reappeared in a basement whose windows lit up at the level of the pavement.

Then, through a bulging grating, its mesh broken in numerous places and twisting its wires in revolt, I saw a tiled floor powdered with white, a row of sacks, an axe, a shovel, and a kneading trough at which two men, without shirts or vests, were working away, deathly pale and yelling out loud, hurling themselves on a big pile of dough which smacked dully when it fell back again on the wood of the trough.

They were grumbling, whining, shouting out inarticulate words, emitting heart-breaking sighs, beating the flaccid paste with great blows. Uhh! uhh! uhh! uhh! smack! slap! u . . . uh! and the putty twisted beneath their fists like the coils of a snake. Their torsos rippled, bulging biceps danced on their arms, big drops of sweat pearled on their foreheads and absorbed the flour accumulated at their temples.

They were slapping away at random like madmen, then, after a final cry wrenched from their entrails, their arms ceased their twirling; the men rubbed their fingers clean against the dough and grabbing their wine bottles, they drank their fill, heads thrown back, Adam's apples jumping madly in the skin of their throats.

With a sudden jerk, they threw themselves forward as they withdrew the bottles from their lips, and on either side of their mouths rivulets ran, thickening in proportion as they merged with the powdery contours of their chins.

Ah, I saw in him the model of your thief and drunkard, Watteau, at last I'd found him, that braggart and guzzler, it was really him, but the vision lasted only a few seconds. The harmonious glug-glug of their throats finished and the bottles being empty, the men went back to their strenuous work at the bake house.

One of them shaped the dough and the other buried it in a brick kiln whose wide open mouth was glowing like a volcano, its birch logs aflame.

O, you worn-out Pierrots, you journeymen bakers! You, who at the hour when swarthy sewer-workers are getting ready to pump out drains, at that solemn moment when one man is picking the lock of the next man's door, and yet another is buying a mistress at a bargain price from someone else, you sweat, grumble and gasp; you begin your war-chant and your cannibal dances around dough that cries out for mercy! Stuff yourselves, howl like wolves and drink like fishes, for you share in the zealous prayers offered up to the God of the poor: Give us this day our daily bread, O white warriors! All wheat and no oats, OK? Amen.

THE CHESTNUT-SELLER

The cobbles jump, loosened by the rolling of trucks and drays; dogs scamper by as fast as they can, men quicken their steps, deafened and blinded by a furious gust of rain and hail. Weathercocks on the tops of houses turn and squeal madly, badly-closed windows moan heartbreakingly, the rusted hinges of gates squeak horribly, while alone on the corner of the street, in a niche next to a wine-merchant's counter, the seller of chestnuts remains impassive, shouting to numbed passers-by: 'Ah-hot, hot chestnuts-ah!'

Whether events are frivolous or grave, this man can always be seen, with his belly to the fire and his face to the wind, as he showers golden-shelled chestnuts into his open-air stove, or as he stirs his sweet chestnuts, simmering in a pot under a rag of blackened canvas. What farces, what tragedies, what prologues of novels, what epilogues of stories he hears these winter mornings, as, cold or icy, the dawn breaks.

There he is, in his booth, lighting his brazier, fanning the coals of the charcoal-pan with his breath, listening all ears to the gossip, the stories, the tittle-tattle of milkmaids and concierges.

Before him pass all the bodily infirmities of the *quartier*, all the vices of the neighbouring houses.

83

Jean-François Raffaëlli's illustration to 'The Chestnut-seller'.

And to the spiteful gossip of the office and the concierge's lodge, revealing the cuckolding of the gentleman who lives on the first floor, specifying the exact hour and day, once a week, when his wife cheated on him, is added the grievances of maids complaining about their wine rations, spinning out the demands of their mistresses, the attempts of their masters, and the exhausting and precocious tastes of their children.

What a chronicle of worthless tittle-tattle he must have amassed since the day he first put on his two-pocketed apron and agreed to slit open those huge canvas sacks, what whining, bitter words he has heard, murmured or barked by couples who brush past him, how many drunken women, how many deceitful lovers, how many winos, and how many loveable rogues he has seen collared by the town's policemen! how many falls, how many cab accidents, how many ribs staved in, limbs disjointed, shoulders dislocated, how many gatherings of the mob in front of pharmacies he has seen, all the while splitting the brown coats of sweet chestnuts with a thrust of his knife, all the while stirring chestnuts that crackle and pop with his wooden spatula!

And yet life is not all rose-coloured in this dog of a job; wind, drizzle, rain and snow have their sport with him; the brazier crackles and whines under the squalls that batter it, scattering billows of smoke that sting the eye and stifle the voice; the charcoal sputters and burns too quickly, customers pass swiftly by, hunching up the collar of their overcoats, no one stops in front of the stall, and behind the unfortunate man, through the windows that separate him from a swimming pool of wine, are regiments of bottles, lined up, bright, inviting, glittering, loud in colour and big of belly, placed on a shelf in front of a mirror. What a temptation, what an allure! Ah, who could put the charm of a measure of wine or tafia rum into words? Don't even look at them, you poor devil, forget the cold, hunger and bottles, and sing with that nasal twang of yours, your obstinate lament: 'Ah-hot, hot chestnuts-ah!'

Go on, toil away in the freezing, freezing cold, blow on your stinking, smoky charcoal, breathe in with open mouth the burning steam from your boiling pan, fill your throat with ashes, soak your boiled hands and your grilled fingers in water, drain the sweet chestnuts, peel the roast chestnuts, stuff your sacks, sell your merchandise to greedy children and dawdling women; shout! philosopher, shout! intone at the top of your voice late into the night, under the cold light of the gaslamps, your miserable refrain: 'Ah-hot, hot chestnuts-ah!'

THE BARBER

You sit yourself down in front of a mahogany cheval-glass whose marble shelf contains hair-gels in small bottles, talcum-powder in blue glass pots, thick horse-hair brushes, steel combs covered in hairs, and an open pot of pomade that has the imprint of an index finger in its yellow putty.

Then the extravagant torture begins.

Body enveloped in a kind of cape, a napkin squeezed like wadding between the flesh of your neck and the collar of your shirt, you feel a slight suffocating sweat break out on your temples, then you receive a shove from a hand which tilts your skull to the right, and the cold of the scissors makes your skin shiver.

To the noisy clicking of steel brandished by the barber, hair scatters in showers, falling into your eyes, lodging on your lashes, sticking to your nostrils, clinging to the corner of your lips which tickle and prick, while another shove of the hand suddenly tilts your skull to the left.

Eyes to the left, eyes to the right, attention! And this farcical to-ing and fro-ing continues, aggravated by the dance of the scissors which manoeuvre around your ears and run over your cheeks, nipping your skin, advancing along your temples in front of your eyes, which squint, dazzled by the steel's bright gleams.

— Would Monsieur like a paper?

— No.

— Fine weather is it not, Monsieur?

— Yes.

— It's years since we've had a winter as mild.

— Yes.

Then a pause; the funereal gardener falls silent. He holds the back of your head now between his two fists and, in defiance of the most elementary rules of hygiene, swings you about with it, first high, then low in quick succession, dangling his beard over your forehead, breathing into your face, examining the mirror to see if your shorn locks are of equal length; he trims a bit here, a bit there, and here again, and then begins to play hide-and-seek with your head which he tries pushing down into your stomach to better judge the effect of his cutting. The torture becomes intolerable. Oh, where are the benefits of science now, the vaunted anaesthetics, its pale morphines, its faithful chloroforms, its pacifying ethers?

But the barber gasps, wheezing like a bull, exhausted by his efforts; then he rushes at your pate again, which he rakes now with a small comb and planes remorselessly with two brushes.

A sigh of discomfort escapes you, as, putting down his two currycombs, he shakes your cape.

— Would Monsieur like his scalp massaged?

— No.

— A shampoo then?

– No.

– Monsieur is making a mistake, it would restore the scalp and get rid of dandruff.

In a faint voice, you end up agreeing to a shampoo, tired, beaten, hoping only to escape from his lair alive.

Then a kind of dew runs, drop by drop, over your forelocks which the man, sleeves rolled, scours. Almost at once this dew, which stinks of orangeade, turns into a foam and, dumbfounded, you catch yourself in the mirror, head covered with a plate of scrambled eggs, out of which stick fat fingers.

The moment has come when the torture is about to reach its ultimate pitch.

Brutally, your head is knocked back and forwards, as if with a racquet, between the arms of the hairdresser who howls and throws himself about; your neck cracks, your eyes leap out of their sockets, a stroke is imminent, madness threatens. In a final flash of commonsense, with a final prayer, you implore the heavens, entreating them on bended knee, to grant a favour: to make you bald, a slap-head!

However, the operation at last comes to an end. You get up, staggering, pale, like someone coming out of a long illness, guided by an executioner who, seizing you by the neck, pushes your head into a wash-basin, sprays it with huge floods of cold water, then squeezes it forcefully with the aid of a towel and carries it back to the chair where, like a piece of scalded meat, it perches immobile and very white.

After enduring these cruel tortures, it only remains to submit to some final disgusting manipulations: a wax treatment is crushed into his palms and plastered over your skull, which is once again flayed by the teeth of his combs.

It is done, you are untied, you stand up, free; you fend off his offers of soap and bottles of *Eau de Lubin*; you pay and you flee as fast as your legs will carry you from this perilous dispensary, but, once outside, the frenzy abates, equilibrium returns, and your thoughts calmly resume their course.

You find you look younger, less middle-aged. At the same time as he was weeding your hair, the barber has by some miracle trimmed off several years; the air seems milder, crisper, a freshness of the spirit blooms, but it fades, alas, almost immediately because an itching caused by the hair cuttings in your shirt makes itself felt. And slowly, nursing a cold, you return home, admiring the eternal heroism of monks whose willing flesh is scraped, night and day, by the rough bristles of their hair-shirts.

IV. LANDSCAPES

THE BIÈVRE

For Henry Céard

Nature is interesting only when sickly and distressed.
I don't deny her prestige and her glory when, with a
fulsome laugh, she cracks open her bodice of sombre
rocks and flaunts her green-nippled breasts in the
sun, but I confess I don't experience before these sap-
induced debaucheries that pitiful charm that a run-
down corner of a great city, a ravaged hillside or a
ditch of water trickling between two lank trees
inspires in me.

Fundamentally, the beauty of a landscape consists
in its melancholy. So the Bièvre, with its air of desperation and the thoughtful look of one who has suffered, charms me more than anything else and I
deplore as the utmost crime the destruction of its
gullies and its trees. This suffering countryside, this
threadbare stream, these ragged plains were all that
were left to us and now they're going to cut them to
pieces. They're going to hang every last patch of
earth out to dry, sell every bowl of water at public
auction, fill in the marshes, level the roads, tear up
the dandelions and the brambles, the whole flora
of rubbish dumps and wasteland. The Rue du

Pot-au-Lait and the Chemin de la Fontaine-à-Mulard, which embrace an entire area choked with slag and rubble, disfigured by sandbags and bits of broken flowerpots, strewn here and there with rotten fruit swarming with flies, with ash and stinking puddles fouled with damp mattress entrails and heaps of slimy filth, will disappear, and that melancholy sight of the artesian well at the Butte aux Cailles and those distant panoramas in which the domes of the Panthéon and the Val-de-Grâce can be seen through a maze of factory chimneys, their two globes purple against the dissolving embers of the clouds, will give place to the idiotic prettiness, to the Sunday-best triteness of new houses!

Ah, the people who decided to sack and pillage these river banks, have they never been moved by the desolate inertia of the poor, by the agonised smile of the sick? Do they only admire nature, then, when it's haughty and in its finery? Have they never, in periods of depression, climbed the hills that overlook the Bièvre? Have they never ever looked at that strange river, that outlet for all kinds of filth, that bilge-water the colour of slate and molten lead, seething here and there with greenish eddies and spangled with cloudy spittle, which gurgles into a sluice-gate and disappears, sobbing, into a hole in a wall? In places, the water seems sclerotic and eaten away with leprosy, it stagnates; then this current of soot stirs again and resumes its progress, slowed down by silt. Over here, bare huts, disreputable-looking sheds, walls rotting, bricks incrusted, a whole assemblage of dismal hues against which, hanging from the casement window of a bedroom, a red cotton eiderdown sounds a piercing note like a call to arms; over there, tanners' shutterless shacks, upturned wheelbarrows, a pitchfork, a rake, coagulated waves of dead wool, a small hill of bark on which a red-crested chicken with a black tail scratches. In the air, fleeces shaken by the wind, scraped hides being stretched, their raw whiteness standing out against the rotting verdigris of wattle fences; on the ground, dropsical buckets, enormous casks in which liquified crusts of leather marinade in dyes the colour of dead leaves and dirty blue; further off still, mangy poplars in a mire of clay, and a mass of escalating hovels, rising one above the other, sordid cattlesheds in which a whole population of brats seethe at windows decked with dirty laundry.

Oh yes, the Bièvre is nothing but a moving rubbish dump, but nevertheless it waters the last remaining poplars in the city. Yes, it exhales the fetid odours of a stagnant pond and the rude stench of the tomb, but throw in a barrel-organ at the foot of one of its trees, spitting out in long gobs the melodies of which its belly is full, conjure up in this vale of tears the voice of a pauper-woman at the water's edge plaintively singing one of those laments picked up by chance at the musichall, a sentimental ballad extolling their darling one and begging for love, and tell me that this wailing doesn't grip you by the entrails, that this sobbing voice isn't the desolate howl of the poor suburbs themselves.

A little sun – and, miracle of heartbroken joys – frogs croak under the rosebushes, a dog stretches, paws spread out, tail in the air, a woman passes by with a small basket in her hand, a man in a cap advances, a stub-pipe between his teeth and, under the watchful eyes of a gang of urchins rolling about in the mud, a ghostly white nag grazes on the wasteland.

The works have begun. The embankment of the Rue de Tolbiac already bars the horizon; soon lime-wash will mask the mottled sores of this ailing *quartier* with its uniform whiteness, and the silhouettes of the skinners' and chamois-makers' open-air driers against the great grey skies will be obscured. Soon that eternal and delightful promenade so beloved by intimists, across a plain furrowed by the industrious and miserable Bièvre as it toils on its way, will be lost forever.

THE POPLAR INN

The plain stretches out, arid and bleak. Great beds of nettles and thistles cover it, broken here and there by the dried-out pools of the dead Bièvre.

To the left, the edge of a pond glitters in the sun like a shard of glass, while the rest stagnates, glazed pistachio-green by duckweed.

In the distance, one or two rickety huts, with mattresses hanging from the windows and flowers planted in milk-cans and old pots; a few trees with sagging branches stand at irregular intervals, exhibiting paralysed arms like beggars, their nodding heads stuttering in the wind, their bowing trunks undernourished by the incurable poverty of the soil.

To the right, a river runs in a thin ribbon the whole length of the plain next to a path that plunges under the arch of a bridge as far as an open postern in some ramparts. Here and there, in less barren soil, marsh-land plants flourish, and eight hardy poplars obscure a cottage whose walls rise up, contrasting pretty streaks of pink plaster against the yellow and green lace-work of leaves. Higher up, close to the roof, you can read this inscription: 'Wine shop', and standing in front of these dainty colours, in front of these arbours hanging over the water, you involuntarily think of the absurd scenery of those rustic inns you see in the theatre; in spite of yourself, you also imagine some dusty sandstone parlour with its walnut cupboard with ironwork fittings, its pewter jugs and its tableware decorated with chickens and flowers; and you think to yourself it would be nice to drink some tart local wine at a corner table, to cut out a big lump of bread from a round home-made loaf, to eat a hearty omelette flecked with little spring onions or larded with bacon, and wash it all down with copious bumpers of drink.

Then you get closer, you cross the motionless stream via a bridge, and this inn, so dapper and welcoming, becomes more threatening, like an animal's lair, like a cut-throat.

The smile of the pink walls has fled; a premature and inelegant agedness has arched the rafters and bent the roof. Standing in front of this hovel, you're instantly put in mind of a ghoulish streetwalker who thieves and slits throats as soon as night falls.

Black paint can be seen beneath the horrible skin of dead plaster like a tattoo, its letters eaten away by the passing of the seasons, spelling out the still intelligible words: 'Sautéed rabbit . . . beers and wines . . . at the meeting of the poplars.' An uneasy silence hovers over this ruin, the old streetlamps that are strung along the road take on a lugubrious, seedy aspect; you shiver at the idea that you might find yourself stuck here, alone, at night.

Seated under an arbour, at a table made out of a plank resting on four bits of wood, you see, after some furious shouting, a serving girl appear at the end of the path, protruding belly, head wrapped in a scarf, eyes sunken, cheeks hollow and covered in freckles.

After having consulted *la patronne*, who hesitates, suspicious, scared of the cops, she brings you a massive, badly-cleaned glass still bearing the traces of other peoples' mouths. She pours out the donkey-piss brewed in that immense building rising above the plain, the old *barrière Blanche* brewery, and then you notice, if you follow the girl's gaze, through the trees to a neighbouring grove, a slumbering workman, cambric shirt open at the neck and baggy trousers pulled tight at the waist by a leather belt. He turns around to swear at the flies and you see the side of his face, hideous, smeared like the walls of a slum with a large stain of blood and wine dregs.

Not a single cart or dray passes by troubling the repose of the deserted lane; only the rolling of the railway echoes, every now and again; clouds of white steam take flight and come to rest in the roof of the arbour. A cock crows, shaking its red crest, flourishing the plumes of its tail, feathered in bottle-green and gold, a flock of ducks making an awful quack-quacking rush headlong into the Bièvre, which awakes and exhales its rotting silage breath; and then, turning towards the ramparts, if you contemplate the horizon scored by the line of fortifications, you are beset by disconsolate and salutary thoughts.

Above you, right above you, covering the sky, the enormous mass of Bicêtre rises up, dominating the whole of Paris like a menace, recalling to mind the disastrous end that awaits the artificial enthusiasms of our jaded senses, the rash over-taxing of our brains, and the sufferings induced by disappointed friendships and ambitions.

Bicêtre, that formidable and grandiose buoy warning of the shallows of the city, completes the desolate image of life already invoked in us by the Bièvre, so joyous and so youthful at Buc, but progressively sicker and blacker as it advances, worn out by the constant labours that are inflicted on it, and then, impotent and putrid, when it has completed its arduous task, it falls, exhausted, into the sewer that sucks it in at a gulp and spits it out again further on, in a forgotten corner of the Seine.

RUE DE LA CHINE

For Jules Bobin

To those who loathe the kind of boisterous joys that are repressed all week and then let loose in Paris on Sundays; to those who want to escape the tedious opulence of the wealthier *quartiers*, Menilmontant will always be a promised land, a Canaan of gentle melancholy.

It is in one of the corners of this *quartier* that the Rue de la Chine, so unique and so charming, unfurls itself. Even though it has been truncated and mutilated by the construction of a hospital, which adds to the discrete and introspective aspect of cottages enclosed by railings and hedges the mournful spectacle of human suffering, wandering around flowerless, tree-less courtyards, this street has nevertheless conserved the joyous appearance of a country lane enlivened by bothies and little gardens.

Such as it is today, this street is the antithesis of the boring symmetry of the new *grands boulevards*, the very opposite of their banal alignment. Everything here is crooked; there are no walls, no bricks, no stones, but on each side, lining an unpaved road furrowed down the middle by a ditch, stretches a

picket fence made from old boat timbers, marbled
with green moss and veneered with golden-brown tar,
which leans, dragging down a whole cluster of ivy,
and almost taking with it a gate, clearly bought in a
lot from some demolition yard, embellished with
mouldings whose delicate grey still shows through
under a brown layer deposited by the successive
touch of dirty hands.

It is only with difficulty that one can make out a
one-storey cottage underneath an embroidery of
Virginia creeper, amid a tangle of valerian, hollyhock
and huge sunflowers whose golden heads are losing
their petals, revealing black bald patches like round
bull's-eyes. Even then, it's invariably behind a hedge
of planks, a zinc water-tank, two pear-tress linked by
a washing line, and a bit of a vegetable garden, containing some squashes with their light yellow flowers,
and some beds of sorrel and cabbages, cut into
squares by the shadows of lacquer-trees and poplars.

In this huge *quartier* where meagre wages doom
women and children to eternal privations, the Rue de
la Chine and those streets which join and cross it,
such as the Rue des Partants and the amazing Rue
Orfila, so fantastic with its windings and its sudden
turns, with its badly squared-off enclosures of trees,
its abandoned summerhouses, its deserted gardens
returning to a state of nature and abounding in
untamed shrubs and wild grasses, give off a unique
note of peace and calm.

It's not like the flat plain of the Gobelins where
the wretchedness of nature is in keeping with the
unrelenting distress of those who inhabit it; here,

under an open sky, it's like a country footpath where most of the people who pass seem to have enough to eat and drink; it's an obscure hideaway dreamt of by artists in quest of solitude; it's a haven beseeched by those pained souls who ask for no more than a welcoming rest far from the crowd; it's a consolation for those disinherited by fate or crushed by life, a comfort born of the inevitable sight of the Tenon hospital, whose upper storeys cleave the sky and whose windows are full of pale faces staring at the open countryside, which they contemplate with the profound and avid eyes of convalescents.

Ah! this street is merciful to the afflicted and charitable to the embittered, because at the thought of those poor people lying in that gigantic hospital, in long wards full of white beds, your own sufferings and complaints seem childish and hollow; and then, at the sight of those cottages hidden down the lane, you dream of a delicious refuge, of a little nest-egg that would allow you to work only when you wanted to and not to have to rush the writing of a book from necessity.

It's true that once returned to the heart of the city, you repeat to yourself, with reason perhaps, that an overwhelming boredom would oppress you in the isolation of such a cottage, in the silence and abandon of such a thoroughfare; and yet, each time that you come to steep yourself again in that quiet and forlorn street, the impression remains the same; it seems that the forgetfulness and peace searched for far away in the contemplation of monotonous beaches finds itself here, at the end of a bus route, in this village footpath lost amid Paris, in the middle of the joyous and mournful tumult of its great poverty-stricken streets.

VIEW FROM THE RAMPARTS
OF NORTH PARIS

From the top of the ramparts you can make out the wonderful and awesome sight of the plains that lie below, worn-out at the foot of the city.

On the horizon, against the sky, tall brick chimneys, round and square, vomit billows of soot into the clouds, while a little further down, barely passing over the flat roofs of workshops covered in bituminised felt and sheet-metal, whistling jets of white steam escape from thin aluminium flue-pipes.

This denuded zone stretches out, swollen with hillocks on which gangs of kids are flying kites made of old newspapers and decorated with the colour pictures that advertisers dole out in shop doorways and at the the ends of bridges.

Near huts whose pale red tiles border limpid lakes of glazed roofs, monumental horsecarts raise their chained shafts to the sky, sheltering here a working-class romance, there a maternal scene in which a child avidly sucks on a dried-up breast. Further off, a goat grazes, tied to a stake; a man sleeps, lying on his back, his eyes hidden by his cap; a seated woman slowly massages her worn-out feet.

A great silence descends over the plain as the

rumble of Paris dies out little by little and the noise from distant factories now reaches you but falteringly. Sometimes, however, like a horrible complaint, you can hear the dull, raucous whistle of trains from the Gare du Nord as they pass, hidden by an embankment planted with acacias and ash trees.

Finally, in the distance, in the far distance, a large white road climbs a hill and loses itself in the sky, its summit crowned by a billow of dust, like a cloud stirred up by an invisible horse-drawn cart, hidden by the curve of the earth.

Towards dusk, when soot-laden clouds roll across the dying day, the landscape becomes boundless and gloomy again; factories become indecisive contours, masses of ink blots against a livid sky; the women and children have all gone home, the plain seems bigger now as, alone in the dusty road, a beggar, the 'hobo' as the street urchins call him, returns to his bed for the night, sweating, exhausted, done in, leaning heavily to one side, sucking his long-empty pipe, followed by his dogs, fantastic, improbable-looking dogs of multifarious bastardies, forlorn dogs accustomed, like their master, to all kinds of famine and every variety of flea.

And it's then, especially then, that the doleful charm of the suburbs makes itself felt; it's especially then that the all-powerful beauty of nature is resplendent, because the landscape is in perfect accord with the profound distress of the families who people it.

Created incomplete, in anticipation of the role that man will assign to her, nature looks to her master for his final, finishing touches: sumptuous buildings that embellish the appearance of *quartiers* inhabited by the rich; cottages that dot a blithe and restful countryside scene with blotches of butter-yellow and cool white; *Parcs-Monceau* that are as tarted-up as the women who parade in them; tall foundries and huge forges that rise up out of landscapes that are as run-down and as imposing as they are, such is the immutable law.

And it's to apply this law, to fulfil the instinct for harmony that obsesses us, that we have delegated engineers to match nature to our needs, to adapt her to our soft and pitiful lives which it's her job to frame and reflect.

V. FANTASIES AND FORGOTTEN CORNERS

THE TALLOW CANDLE: A PROSE BALLAD

For Gabriel Thyébaut

When Carcel lamps were all the fashion illuminating the rooms of well-off families, you alone lit those attic rooms in which pre-pubescent pauper girls would calculate, in a daydream, the value of their budding charms: O tallow candle, sputtering candle!

Then the body begins to decay, ripened by dissipation; already there are folds of fat across the belly and the breasts sag; the money earned by the sweat of her charms dries up and hunger beckons. It's no longer Madam Julia, it's Old Mother Jules, who gets drunk and snuffs you out: O tallow candle, sputtering candle!

But now the sight of you awakens in me more personal, more intimate memories; in front of your wick, which mushrooms and reddens in a lake of tallow, I recall my childhood, those long winter evenings when, tired by my screams and my tears, my mother would send me to the kitchen to sit next to the maid, and she would spell out loud from a big book of fairytales: O tallow candle, sputtering candle!

Then these distant recollections also begin to fade, little by little, and pitiful memories come back to me of ideals forever shattered. Now, I see in my mind those gloomy lodgings where, awaiting the arrival of a mistress, I would stare, stupefied, ears pricked, telling myself over and over again that she would never come, as the sewer flies danced and burned in your flame: O tallow candle, sputtering candle!

If today, usurped by paraffin- and oil-lamps, you are forsaken even by the poor, at least you've been flattered as never queen was, O smoking candle! Rembrandt, Gerrit Dou and Godfried Schalcken have celebrated you in immortal prints; they have used you to illuminate the snowy pink skin, the straw-coloured fingers of those Flemish maids who shelter you with their hands from the wind's breath: O tallow candle, sputtering candle!

Envoy

Princess, let others sing of the moon's phosphorescent gleam, of the lantern's red flame, of the gaslamp's yellow light, it's you alone I love, you alone I want to exalt, ideal illumination for the paintings of the old masters: O tallow candle, sputtering candle!

DAMIENS

For Robert Caze

The intensity of these painful pleasures wrenched a cry from my throat; my ears were full of buzzing and my eyes were closed; it seemed to me that my nerves were churning and my head was going to split open; I almost lost consciousness; then, after a while, my senses came back to life – hearing first – and in the distance, the far distance, as if in a dream, I heard a flush of water and the sound of a door.

Eventually, I opened my eyes and looked around me; I was alone, in a bedroom hung with red wall-paper, with muslin curtains veiling the cross of the windows. Above a sofa covered in crocheted lace was a round mirror set at a slight incline against the wall, and at this angle it reflected the part of the room to which my back was turned. I could see a chimney-breast surmounted by a clock with a broken pendulum and candleholders with no candles in them, and on either side of a marble washbasin were two very low, splay-fronted armchairs positioned under two burning gas-lamps that were hissing in the silence of the room.

Like a bed of dazzling tulips arrayed around a

clear pool, flames of colour were kindling in a circle around the mirror, in the bevelling that ran inside the gilded wood of the frame. My hypnotised eyes were burning, I wanted to tear them away from this rim of scorching flowers and plunge them, so as to refresh them, in the water of the mirror; but in the midst of the images of furniture that filled it, a fleck of gold leapt out from the chimneybreast and sparkled, stinging my overtired pupils with its harsh fires.

Suddenly, with a supreme effort, I averted my eyes and raised them above my head towards the heavens, beseeching a renewal of energy, a resurgence of strength.

Then I saw a hideous sight.

Motionless on a bed, his legs naked and his feet contorted, his rigid arms stuck to his body, lay a man, his night-shirt gathered up over his knees. His swimming eyes seemed ready to drip, liqueur-like, down the folds of his cheeks; his haggard features, pale and gaunt, and a thin nose joined to the mouth by deep wrinkles, betrayed irreparable anxieties, inconsolable sorrows, laborious tragedies.

And over the skin of this still breathing corpse ran a slow shudder.

It seemed to me that, somewhere or other, I had already beheld this unfortunate, dying on a bed. I was vainly wandering in the mists of my memory when suddenly, as if through a clearing, my thoughts clarified. It was in the Rue Bonaparte, in the window of a print-seller; there, amid a jumble of images, a simple old engraving had taken me by surprise. It depicted a man stretched out on a mattress, bound hand and foot with straps, dead eyes rolling in his ravaged face. Close by, soldiers sporting perukes and tricorn hats, dressed in officers' jerkins and culottes buckled at the knee, were standing to attention, swords in their fists, while behind them two judges in clerical habits were staring, pens in hand, with a contemplative air at the vault of the prison cell in which the scene was taking place.

And in a flash, I remembered the title written in pencil under the old print: *Damiens.* And my thoughts went back through the ages to that man who had so childishly attempted to kill a King with a penknife. I attended the solemn interrogation brought to mind by the engraving, then I imagined the guilty man being quartered, as indeed he was, by four horses, on the Place de Grève. And I began to tremble, for the image I had seen above my head was my own reflection in a mirror fixed to the top of the bed on which I was lying: face distorted, eyes sunken, arms rigid, cleaving to the body, night-shirt gathered above the knee.

The sound of a door and the coming-and-going of footsteps broke the spell of the obsession that was haunting me. I sat up in bed, shattering the pitiful portrait mirrored by the ceiling of the bed, re-assuming my own facial expression, and finally re-entering my own skin.

I got up and, going over to the chimney, on the mantelpiece of which shone a golden twenty-franc piece I had put there beforehand, I smiled to myself and thought:

The physical analogy I conjured up between the

posture of the clumsy assassin and my own is, from the spiritual point of view, perhaps even more just.

For in effect had I not endured, morally-speaking, a torture identical to that which was inflicted on the body of the regicide?

Had I not myself been pulled and jerked on a spiritual Place de Grève by four differing reflections, quartered as it were: firstly by thoughts of contemptible lust; then by an immediate disillusion of desire on entering the room; next, by penitential regret for the money spent; and finally, by that expiatory feeling of anguish these fraudulent sensual contracts, once committed, inevitably induce.

ROAST MEAT: A PROSE POEM

For Alexis Orsat

It's the spurious roast beefs and deceptive legs of lamb cooked in restaurants that engender fantasies of cohabitation in the embittered minds of old bachelors.

The moment has come for the pink, lukewarm, damp smelling meat to turn your stomach. Seven o'clock strikes. In his customary chop-house, the bachelor looks for the table at which he normally sits, and is pained to see that it is already occupied. He takes his wine-stained serviette from the rack hanging on the wall and, after having exchanged bland formalities with those at neighbouring tables, he runs through the unchanging menu and sits himself down, morose, in front of some soup which the waiter brings, washing in it as he does so – as he does every evening – his thumb.

In order to rekindle his lost appetite, the modest expense of his dinner now has to be inflated with wasteful extras, with heavily vinaigretted salads and half a siphon of Seltzer water.

It's then, after having gulped down his soup, and while sliding stringy slices of dried-up sirloin around

Jean-François Raffaëlli's illustration to 'Roast meat: a prose poem'.

in a mundane brown sauce, that the bachelor seeks to assuage the horrible disgust that grips his throat and makes his stomach heave.

An initial fantasy obsesses him as he looks, without reading, at the newspaper he has pulled out of his pocket. He recalls a young girl he could have married ten years ago: he sees himself wedded to her, eating robust meats and drinking honest burgundies, but then the opposite image immediately rises up, and all the stages of a hideous marriage unroll before his afflicted spirit. He imagines himself in the bosom of his new family, taking part in the ceaseless exchange of inane ideas and in interminable games of lotto, relieved only by the old nicknames given to the numbers. He sees himself longing for his bed, but then having to submit, once he's lying down, to the repeated advances of a bad-tempered spouse; he sees himself dressed in black in the middle of a ball in winter, prevented from taking the little nap he was just settling down to by the furious glance of his dancing wife; he hears himself reproached on his return for his sullen attitude as he lounged by the door, finally, he suddenly sees himself treated by the world as a confirmed cuckold . . . and the distracted diner shudders and eats with more resignation a mouthful of the sickening stew congealing on his plate.

But as he chews the insipid, leathery meat, as he endures the acidic belches provoked by the Seltzer water, the bachelor's melancholy returns and he dreams, this time, of a decent sort of woman who, tired of the hazards of life, would like a more secure future; he dreams of a woman already mature, in whom the pangs of love have run their course, of a motherly, unsophisticated companion who, in exchange for food and shelter, would put up with all his old habits, all his old fads.

No family to visit, no dances to submit to, the table laid at the same hour every day in his own home, no fears of being deceived by his wife, little chance, what's more, of giving birth to brats who squeal under the pretext of cutting their teeth . . . and, hastened by his ever increasing disgust for eating out, the idea of a mistress becomes more pressing, more fixed in his mind, and the bachelor succumbs, goes down with all hands, seeing in a distant mirage a joyous roasting jack, red as the sun, in front of which slowly revolves, oozing huge drops of fat, an almighty rump-steak.

It's the spurious roast beefs and deceptive legs of lamb cooked in restaurants that engender fantasies of cohabitation in the embittered minds of old bachelors.

A CAFÉ

Close to a railway station, on the corner of a public square, there's a museum of natural history in which you can gamble and in which you can drink.

The place is sleepy and placid. It's a café with an unchanging clientele, no passing trade, a café whose door only opens to familiar faces that provoke cheers and laughter on their entrance; it's a café where ten *rentiers* meet every evening around a table, exchanging commonplace insights on politics as they play cards, and interest themselves interminably in the pregnancies of the *patronne* and of her cat; it's a bar where everyone owns a pipe with his name enamelled on it, a New Year's Day present from the waiter, who is dozing as usual, his nose in a newspaper, and who throws out a miserable and listless 'There . . .' whenever anyone asks him for another beer.

The appearance of the room is strange; above Chesterfield sofas upholstered in chocolate-brown leather, two glass cases, their grey wood panelling set off with pale blue moulding, rise up the length of the walls, crammed from top to bottom with stuffed, painted birds.

The bottom shelf of one of them, situated opposite the entrance, holds swans with yellow wooden beaks, their bellies bursting with straw and shrunken, unevenly stuffed necks sketching white S's, as well as several sacred ibis, their feet waxed and polished, and with heads of that dirty red that red-currant jam turns bread.

Then, on shelves ranged up to the ceiling are stacked innumerable birds, some big, some medium, some small, some crooked, some bandy-legged, some erect; a variety of winged creatures, some with a good-natured air, some like ugly customers bearing beaks curved like pick-axes or elongated like the point of a nail, and others with beaks that look like needles or like sugar-tongs, and all have the same rosette-like eyes, orange and black, the same fixed, idiotic stare, all have feathers the colour of nutmeg and pepper, horribly faded plumage and the awkward, stupidly self-satisfied bearing of actors.

Seen closer to, the large and gloomy stain cast over the glass cabinets by this mass of mournful hues dissolves, revealing as it does so, ranged without distinction of kinship or caste in a beggarly and verminous promiscuity, game-cocks with beaks like syringes, staring with vicious, ill-natured faces at some little quails whose eyes, sweet and imploring, are raised to the heavens, and all lost amid dynasties of bar-tailed godwits and bitterns, amid entire families of herons standing on one leg waiting for who knows what, dreaming perhaps of unbelievable fish, stuffed like themselves.

Three birds with feathers that once quivered with vibrant tones are, however, trying to break up the tearful harmony of this tableau: a fledgling of a dirty sulphur colour that has lost its label; a roller paralysed in mid-frolic in its awful, faded green costume; and a sentimental and lyrical pheasant, its golden, fire-red feathers now extinguished.

Despite the sad and burlesque appearance of its occupants, uniformly arranged in a row, standing to attention, over-varnished feet glued to those black wooden stands or perched on branches decorated with imitation moss, this cabinet contrasts magnificently with the other, which seems to be the prop room for an aviary in a melodrama.

For there, sure enough, on a series of small boards, a whole raggle-taggle of sinister, ugly beasts is gathered: groups of owls shrouded under layers of dust, beaks curved like secateurs, hunched wings the colour of tinder and ash, gloomy screech-owls, pretentiously labelled under the Latin name *Strix nebulosa*, screech-owls from the Urals with the thoughtful look of the blind, eagle-owls with sardonic and fierce faces, and stupid, melancholy ravens, like seedy gentlemen shivering beneath their thin suits of black feathers.

A little higher up, this cemetery of winged creatures is rounded off with a set of beasts that must have been dragged out of an auction room, in a lot bought at a bankruptcy sale: jackdaws and crows, more amiable and dapper than their neighbours, at whom they stare in disgust; a flock of old kites, flabby and grumpy, strutting about in their moth-eaten rags; a clan of falcons with the gait of rogues and braggarts; and bad-tempered buzzards scowling officiously.

And the patron of this establishment, the creator of this café-museum, seems to have been in the grip of an *idée-fixe*; not content to have stuffed his cupboards with the carcasses of birds, preserved in spices and camphor, he has also decorated his windows with yellow blinds like ungummed sticking-plasters, bearing, by chance no doubt, the arms of the city of the Hague: a swan holding a serpent in its beak; he has wrapped pythons, glazed and stuffed with wadding, around the columns of his bar, his ceiling is carpeted with indistinct sturgeons attached by hooks, and with huge flat-fish like enormous combs, and finally, like a prize specimen, with an old crocodile, its legs splayed, its open mouth, patched with shoe-leather and containing neither teeth nor stumps, invaded by an army of flies that work away and dung, swarming in between the edges of its jaws.

The astonishment of the waiter when the curious consult him about the origin of, and the idea behind, this café, is extreme. Thinking that you're making a fool of him, he at first keeps silent, then, realising the innocence of the people who are questioning him, he replies, pityingly and contemptuously: Oh, there's an even finer one at Bar-le-Duc!

And content with this response, as you finish emptying your glass you take in the ugliness of all these birds with a final glance, feeling no desire at all to go and visit Bar-le-Duc, thinking rather, in front of these tables full of old *rentiers*, their noses stuck in their cards, motionless as if preserved in this funereal atmosphere, of a jerry-built Versailles, of a bargain-basement Egypt, of a necropolis of fowls and men.

RITORNELLO

Dead, the man who beat her black and blue, left her three children, and died sodden with absinthe.

Ever since, she flounders in the mud, pushes her barrow, shouts at the top of her voice: Get it here! Get it here!

She is unutterably ugly. She is a monster: above a wrestler's neck rolls a red, grimacing face, hollowed out with bloodshot eyes and embossed with a nose whose flaring nostrils, like tobacco pouches, swarm with spots and blemishes.

They have a good appetite, those three children; it's for them that she flounders in the mud, pushes the barrow, shouts at the top of her voice: Get it here! Get it here!

A neighbouring woman happens to die:

Dead, the man who beat her black and blue, left her three children and died sodden with absinthe.

The monster doesn't hesitate to take them in.

They have a good appetite, those six children! To work! To work! Without cease, without respite, she flounders in the mud, pushes the barrow, shouts at the top of her voice: Get it here! Get it here!

THE ARMPIT

For Guy de Maupassant

There are questionable smells, ambiguous as a shout from a dark alleyway. Certain working-class *quartiers* of Paris emit them in summer when you pass a group of female workers. Negligence, and the sheer fatigue of arms that have sweated over arduous work, explain the pungent scent of goat that rises from their sleeves.

Stronger and coarser still, I have traced this fragrance to the countryside, to a team of women passing in the midday sun after spreading hay. It was excessive, terrible; it stung your nostrils like a flask of ammonia, or rather it gripped you, irritating the mucus membranes with a musky, gamey smell, like wild duck cooked in olives and the sharp odour of shallots. But in truth, this emanation had nothing repugnant or vile about it; it harmonised with the strong smells of the countryside, like something expected; it was a pure note, the sultry cry of the human animal complementing the pungent melody of livestock and of woodland.

But let's leave all that; after all, I don't want to concern myself with slovenly armpits, with bestial

126

humanity, with the rabble or with the rustic, who care little for washing and have little time to rest. I want simply to speak of the exquisite and divine scent prepared by the women of our cities, wherever they get overheated, whether in a ballroom in winter, or in the street in summer.

Unfiltered by cambric or linen, which refines it or disperses it as a handkerchief does when you pour cologne on it, the perfume given off by these female arms is less clarified, less delicate, less pure in an open ball-gown. Then, an aroma of valerianate of ammonia and of urine is at times brutally accentuated, and sometimes even a light fragrance of prussic acid, a faint hint of bruised or overripe peach blends with a whiff of perfumes and powders.

Yet it's at this moment that the *Parisienne* is at her most enchanting, at this moment when, under a leaden sky, during one of those spells when, stifled by a threatening storm, she walks, sheltered under her umbrella, sweating like a water-cooler, eyes deadened by the heat, skin damp, face languid and drained, that her scent escapes, ameliorated by the filter of her underclothes, at one and the same time both deliciously impudent and shyly delicate!

Never were women more desirable than at these moments, with their Oxford wool dresses moulding their bodies from top to toe, clinging to them like the damp chemises that imprison them underneath. The appeal of this aromatic, exuded from under their arms, is less insolent, less cynical than in the dance-hall, when they are uncovered, but it uncages the beast in man more readily.

As diverse as hair colour and as undulating as the curls that conceal it, the odour of the armpit could be analysed *ad infinitum*; no aroma has more nuances, its range traverses the whole keyboard of the sense of smell, sometimes hinting at the insistent scents of seringia and elder-flower, sometimes recalling the soft perfume of one's fingers after having rolled and smoked a cigarette.

Daring and occasionally wearying in the brunette and the raven-haired, sharp and wild in the redhead, the armpit of the blonde is as dizzying and heady as certain sweet wines, and you could almost say that this perfectly matches the way in which their lips dole out their kisses: more forceful and angry in the dark-haired, more enthusiastic, more intimate perhaps, in the blonde.

But whether the colour of the hair concealed under the arms is dark or light, whether their tufts are wavy like a moustache or curly like thin shavings of mahogany or rosewood, it has to be admitted that mother nature is provident and far-sighted; she has distributed these spice-boxes in order to salt and season the stew of love, which habit renders so tasteless and indigestible even to those resigned to their conjugal duties, men who have knowingly consented to surrender to the marriage bed their positive preference for peace and a regular diet.

LOW TIDE

In a boutique on the Rue Legendre, in the Batignolles district, a whole series of women's busts with no heads or legs, with curtain-hooks instead of arms and percaline skin, starkly-coloured in greyish-browns, garish pinks and harsh blacks, are aligned in a row, impaled on spikes or placed on tables.

At first, you think of a morgue in which the torsos of decapitated cadavers are standing; but soon the horror of these amputated corpses fades and more suggestive reflections come to mind, because that subsidiary charm of a woman, her bosom, is here displayed, faithfully reproduced by the incomparable dressmakers who have constructed these busts.

Over here are the bony chests of the tom-boy, small swellings beaded with drops of rosé wine, dainty blisters punctured by dwarfish tips. And these budding pubescences arouse in us that licentious impatience for things begun and of which one desires the sequel.

Over there are the breasts of old, positively skinny women, little turnips dabbed with lilac, planed boards of knotted pine; and over there are the griddle-cakes of the pious, worn down by scandal-mongering and prayer, and there, the gaiter-buttons of the old maid, crushed and flattened by celibacy. To one side, further off, the wear and tear of life begins to show itself, its misfortunes made visible in the form of flabby puddings, limp brioches, barren mitts forever downcast by the disasters of breast-feeding, forever disfigured by ruinous debaucheries.

But then, still further along the tables in the boutique, these beginnings of growth and these wastings of chastity and lust give way to prudent *bourgeoises* with half-full bodices, to medium-sized busts with nipples of hydrangea blue, purple studs ringed by haloes of dark brown.

Then, after the barely perceptible plumpness of the neither fat nor thin, after the charm of the fuller-figured, corpulence becomes more noticeable, and suddenly a terrifying series of the bloated and the obese begins to assert itself: the enormous dewlaps, the brick-red or bronze-tipped jugs of stout nannies, the one-eyed wine-skins of female colossi, the formidable lardy bladders of roly-poly women, the monstrous gourds – gourds with olive eyes – of ageing pot-bellies!

Looking at this expanse of busts revealed as if by a low tide, this Curtius Museum of breasts, you think vaguely of the underground galleries in which repose the antique sculptures of the Louvre, where the same, eternally repeated torso brings joy to men who contemplate it, yawning, on rainy days.

But how great a difference there is between those inhuman marbles and the bonded percaline of these terrifying specimens. The Greek bosom, carved according to a formula laid down by the taste of centuries, is now dead; nothing in us is stirred by these conventional forms, sculpted in a cold material that wearies our eyes. And then, it has to be said, how disgusting it would be if the *Parisienne*, as she stripped, was to flaunt such impeccable charms and you had to make merry, on days of need, with such monotonous busts and breasts as these!

How superior to those mournful statues of Venus are these lifelike dressmakers' mannequins; how much more insinuating are these upholstered busts, the sight of which evokes interminable reveries — debauched reveries in front of ephebic tits and bruised dugs; charitable reveries in front of aged mammaries shrivelled by chlorosis or bloated by fat — because they bring to mind the sufferings of those unfortunate women who despairingly watch their bodies dry up or swell out, who sense their husband's impending indifference, the imminent desertion of their keeper, the final disarmament of charms that had enabled them to conquer in those necessary battles fought over man's contracted wallet.

OBSESSION

For Edmond de Goncourt

Consolidateds are up, industrial securities holding, Panama falling and Suez steady. Crossword and cryptic puzzles; correct solutions: *Paul Ychinel, le père Spicace, Astre à Caen, Lady Scorde, Miss Tigry*, Oedipuses of the Café du Grand-Balcon! Rowland's oil of macassar and Guyot's tar. Russian corn cures and Wlinsi paper. Dry-nurse seeks employment. An End To Baldness! Fresh Growth Guaranteed Or Your Money Back. Judge For Yourself! Malleron. Secret afflictions, Ulcers, Discharges, Dandruff: Chable, Emmanuel, Péchenet, Albert!

* * *

These advertisements, read on the back page of a torn newspaper that I find in the bottom of my pocket as I stand by the side of a road, with the countryside stretching away into the distance, demolish the much-desired feeling of calm that was growing within me. This piece of paper drags me back to Paris, and the cares of my present life, from which I had at last broken free, now return.

Fatally, I count the days. Another week and I'll have to buckle up the trunks again, go into town and search for a cab. Then there'll be the deafening grain-hopper of a railway carriage, stuffed with a mass of creatures whose faces fill one with repugnance; there'll be the return to Paris, and the following day, after a disoriented sleep, will begin again all the disgusts of a life battered by the painful prostitution of one's ideas, by the continually mistaken conjectures of one's senses, and by the lively antipathies one has to try and overcome in order to eat and pay the rent.

Oh, to think that there will always be a Before and an After, but never a Now that endures.

And then memories of previous homecomings begin to stir; I recall the melancholy of train station arrivals, and the forgotten stench of the streets; I recall the spiritual malaise induced by a cold, empty apartment and the impossibility, in the days that follow, of being able to sit alone in public and avoid the unbearably irritating chatter spewed out by a mob that can't keep quiet.

It all comes back to me; I tally up the journeys made trying to raise money; I see in my mind the enthusiastic offers, the almost-polite rejection letters, the copious amounts of advice, the whole turgid sewer of inexorable existence into which I must plunge once more.

And besides it's pleasant stretching out on this bank by the road-side; work in the fields is coming to an end, interrupted by nightfall, and the old church is silhouetted against the horizon, above a valley which looks bigger and deeper in the shadows; through the nave, through the clear windows facing me, I can see the dark mists in the sky pass by.

But the vision of the present doesn't stick in my mind; so I try to lead my thoughts back to the past, to recall the peaceful feelings experienced only the night before on a deserted hill-top, where, amid blocks of granite, juniper bushes thrust their green thorns and blue berries towards the sun.

But I can't moor my memory in this image either, which fades as soon as it's evoked. In the end, I endeavour to retire into myself, to scrutinise myself, to staunch the cares that are welling up inside me, to repress the anguish I feel springing forth. But I fall back on specious beliefs, subtle reasonings and insidious hopes in vain. The poor Now, finally conjured up, has already passed; the siesta of my sufferings is over and all the odium, all the contempt with which I've been showered awakes and sounds a furious reveille; and all the while I'm beset and dominated by the haunting headlines of that odious newspaper.

* * *

Consolidateds are up, industrial securities holding, Panama falling and Suez steady. Crossword and cryptic puzzles; correct solutions: *Paul Ychinel, le père Spicace, Astre à Caen, Lady Scorde, Miss Tigry,* Oedipuses of the Café du Grand-Balcon! Rowland's oil of macassar and Guyot's tar. Russian corn cures and Wlinsi paper. Dry-nurse seeks employment. An

End To Baldness! Fresh Growth Guaranteed Or Your Money Back. Judge For Yourself! Malleron. Secret afflictions, Ulcers, Discharges, Dandruff: Chable, Emmanuel, Péchenet, Albert!

VI. STILL LIFES

THE HERRING

For Alfred Alavoine

Thy robe, O herring, is a palette composed of setting suns, the patina of old copper, the burnished gold of Cordoba leather, and the sandalwood and saffron hues of autumn leaves!

Thy head, O herring, blazes like a golden helmet, and your eyes look like black nails hammered into circles of copper!

All these sad and mournful shades, all these radiant and cheerful shades, by turns subdue and then illuminate your scaly robe. Next to Judea bitumens and Cassel earths, burnt umbers and Scheele's greens, Van Dyck browns and Florentine bronzes, tints of rust and dead leaves, shine verdigrised golds, amber yellows, orpiments, sumach ochres, chromiums and Mars yellow in all their splendour!

O shimmering and tarnished kipper, when I contemplate thy coat of mail I think of Rembrandt's paintings, I see once more his superb heads, his sunlit flesh, the way his jewels glitter against black velvet, I see once more his flashes of light in the night, his trails of golden dust in the shadows, his suns dawning through darkened archways.

THE EPINAL PRINT

For Eugène Montrosier

It was a small town near Brussels in the Duchy of Brabant; its houses defined by a line of pale ink that could just be made out against a grey paper sky.

There were gabled houses, a church surmounted by a cross, and amid the rooftops, some serrated like sawblades, some like pepper-pots, some like upside-down cornets and some like candle-snuffers, a tower pierced with loopholes.

There was also a large, flesh-coloured turret, capped with a red roof. This turret formed the corner of an inn on the yellow balcony of which a lady, wearing a frilled ruff and a dress of the same red as the roof of the turret, was leaning.

The little town seemed to be in a state of commotion, for there were no fewer than six people in the square questioning an old man. Two were fine gentlemen, dressed in costumes of the Louis XIII period, one of whom, a fat man with a chubby, baby-face, the face of a real boon companion, a right joker, a true good-time Gaul, was beardless, dressed in a jerkin of the brightest red vermillion with a big collar whose white tips were bleeding into the red of his tunic, and in one hand he was holding a cap of grey felt, spotted with the blue that had served to paint his breeches, while with the other he was pointing out to the old man a mug of beer, which was foaming on a green-daubed table adorned with four yellow legs. The legs of this table must have been luminous, because they were spreading large patches of the same colour all around them.

The old man was refusing chubby-cheeks' offer, and his fingers, which he was holding out in front of him as if to fend off the gifts of Artaxerxes, were stained with purple where they were touching his tunic.

The other gentleman was thinner, and above his mouth he sported a pair of small moustaches. Apart from this difference, the two men strongly resembled each other. Both had pinkish complexions, with lips, eyes, ears, and hair, everything merging into the same colour; in places the colour had even leapt off their faces and was running over clothes and houses. The man with the moustaches was smiling with an amiable air and held in his hand a large hat, the yellow of which was bleaching his fingers. Both were saying to the old man who seemed very old and very tired and who was sordidly dressed in an old scarlet cap, a leather apron, a green coat that was flowered with brown and red patches, flecked with darns and seams and forked at the bottom like a crayfish's tail, and a huge blue cloak over which fell in torrents a long beard that was so white, so white one would have said that clouds of vapour were coming out of his mouth and nose and rolling in waves to the ground:

– Good day, master, grant us the pleasure of your company for a short while.

And he, who seemed so old and so tired, was answering them:

– Messieurs, I suffer a terrible misfortune, I can never stop, I walk incessantly.

And they replied in unison:

– Come into this inn, sit yourself down, come and drink a mug of cool beer; we'll entertain you the best we can.

And the old man repeated:

– In truth, Messieurs, I am overwhelmed by your generosity, but I cannot sit down, I must remain standing.

At this, the fine gentlemen were astonished and the fat one said to him:

– We should be curious to know your age.

And the thin one added:

– Are you not the old man about whom we have heard so much, the one they call the Wandering Jew.

And the old man whose beard was so white, so white that you would have said that clouds of vapour were coming out of his mouth and nose, answered them:

– Isaac Laquedem is my name and I am one thousand eight hundred years old; yes, my children, I am the Wandering Jew.

Then he told them of his long travels around the world, his incessant journeying over vale and hill, over land and sea, and when he had finished his lamentable story he cried out:

– Time is pressing, goodbye Messieurs, and for your kindness I thank you once again.'

And he leaned on his long cane, while a small angel, dressed in a red robe and with green wings, a sword in one hand and a yellow streak of gamboge escaping from the other which he was holding open, was making a sign to him to walk, always to walk!

This angel hovered over the small town near Brussels in the Duchy of Brabant. He hovered above the houses defined by a line of pale ink that could just be made out against a grey paper sky.

He hovered above the gabled houses and the church surmounted by a cross, above the rooftops, some serrated like sawblades, some like pepper-pots, some like upside-down cornets and some like candle snuffers, and above the tower pierced by loopholes.

VII. PARAPHRASES

Plate I: *Hommage à Goya* (1885), Odilon Redon. *Dans mon rêve, je vis au Ciel un VISAGE DE MYSTERE* (In my dream, I saw a FACE OF MYSTERY in the Sky).

Plate II: *Hommage à Goya* (1885), Odilon Redon. *La FLEUR du MARECAGE, une tête humaine et triste* (The MARSH FLOWER, a sad, human head).

Plate III: *Hommage à Goya* (1885), Odilon Redon. *Un FOU, dans un morne paysage* (A MADMAN, in a bleak landscape).

Plate IV: *Hommage à Goya* (1885), Odilon Redon. *Il y eut aussi des ETRES EMBRYONNAIRES* (There were also EMBRYONIC BEINGS).

Plate V: *Hommage à Goya* (1885), Odilon Redon. *Un étrange JONGLEUR* (A strange JUGGLER).

Plate VI: *Hommage à Goya* (1885), Odilon Redon. *Au réveil j'aperçus la DEESSE de l'INTELLIGIBLE, au profil sévère et dur* (On awaking I saw the severe and stern profile of the GODDESS of the INTELLIGIBLE).

Marsh Flower. Odilon Redon 1885.

Portrait of J.-K. Huysmans by Odilon Redon.

NIGHTMARE

At first it was an enigmatic face, dolorous and proud, that loomed out of shadows here and there pierced by shafts of daylight: the head of a Chaldean mage, of an Assyrian king, of old Sennacherib brought back to life, watching, desolate and pensive, as the river of ages flows by, a river ever more swollen by the turgid streams of human stupidity.

He places a thin, noble hand, like the slender hand of a young Spanish *infante* on his lips, and opens an eye across which seem to pass the eternal sorrows that have been handed down, and that have reverberated in the souls of men and women, from the time of Genesis. Is this the primitive shepherd of men contemplating the parade of his immortal flocks who fight and massacre each other over a tuft of grass or a crust of bread? Is this the face of immemorial Melancholy who at last admits, before Joy's avowed impotence, the absolute uselessness of everything? Or is it the mythical figure of Truth, revived once more, who recognises, beneath the various masks and cheap finery of his passage through life, the same man, afflicted with the same virtues and the same vices, the same man, whose original ferocity has in no way been ameliorated by the force of time, but has simply been dissimulated behind that grace of civilised peoples, a profound and subtle hypocrisy?

Whichever it was, this mysterious face haunted me; in vain I tried to scrutinise its far-off gaze; in vain I tried to sound out a face that purely personal sufferings could not have furrowed in such a way; but the hieratic and dolorous image disappeared, and, to that modern vision of ancient times, succeeded a ghastly landscape, a swamp of stagnant water, dismal and black; this water stretched as far as the horizon, bounded by a sky like a huge panel made from a single piece of ebony, without the Milky Way's white solder-spatter, without the silver screw-heads of the stars.

From out of this shadowy water, under that opaque sky, suddenly sprang the monstrous stalk of an inconceivable flower.

You might have said it was a wand of rigid steel on which metallic leaves, shiny and hard, were growing. Then buds sprouted out, like tadpoles, like nascent foetuses' heads, like small whitish balls with no nose, no eyes and no mouth; finally, one of these buds, luminous as if smeared with a phosphorescent oil, split, swelling up to form a pale head that swayed silently in the watery night.

An immense and wholly personal sadness emanated from this pale flower. There was in the expression of its features, at one and the same time, the heartbreak of an ageing Pierrot, of an old acrobat mourning his flabby loins, the distress of an ancient lord consumed by spleen, of an attorney convicted of bankruptcy scams, of an old judge who, in the wake of elaborate crimes, has ended up in the courtyard of a house of correction.

I asked myself from what excessive ills this pallid face could have suffered and what solemn expiation caused it to shine over the water, like an illuminated buoy, like a lantern announcing to Life's passengers the lamentable reefs hidden beneath the waves they were going to have to plough across as they scudded into the Future.

But I didn't even have the time to shape the necessary reply to this question I'd asked myself. The terrible flower of ignominy and suffering, the fantastical and living lotus had wilted and its phosphoric halo had faded. And in place of the pale attorney, the bloodless clown, and the ghastly lord, was substituted a vision no less horrible.

It was of a sheet of water, diseased and cloudy, but with no sky this time, a sheet of water filling a huge plain, a gigantic aqueduct supported by columns, like those on the Dhuis and the Vanne. A sepulchral silence fell from the arches; dreary daylight filtered through the frosted glass of hidden portholes; a wind as if from an ice-tunnel shivered your marrow and, in this solitude, an intense, irresistible fear nailed you, breathless, to the stone seat which ran like a quay the whole length of this lifeless water.

Then, from under these fearsome, silent arches, strange beings suddenly sprang up. A head, with no body, hovered, whirring like a top, a head pierced by an enormous Cyclopean eye, complete with a mouth like that of a skate, separated by a wide groove from

151

a nose, the filthy nose of a bailiff, stuffed with snuff! And this white, scalded head was coming out of a kind of skillet, and was radiating its own light, illuminating the waltz of other almost amorphous heads, some like embryos hinting at skulls, some like blurred infusoria, vague flagellates, indefinite monera and bizarre protoplasms like Haeckel's Bathybius, though less gelatinous and less unformed.

And then this formation of living matter disappeared in its turn, this vile species of head faded away, and the obsession with this motionless water finally ceased.

There was a short respite in this nightmare. Then suddenly, a sun, inky-black to the core, emerged from the shadows, bursting, like a Grand Cross medal, with unequal but regularly spaced rays of gold. At the same time flower petals fell from some unknown space, bulbs in which imperceptible pupils squinted bounced around like billiard-balls, and a coffee-maker's sieve remained suspended in the air, beneath which undulated the bare arm of a superhuman juggler with terrifying eyes, as if shaped and enlarged by surgery, round eyes with a pupil stuck on like the boss of a cartwheel.

There was in this man who was conjuring with planets, grocer's implements and flowers, the cruel air of a tough Gaul, the imperious countenance of a bloodthirsty bard; and the awfulness of his dilated eyes, like rings of iron, hypnotised you and made your hair stand on end.

Finally, there was a lull; the mind, carried away by these hallucinations, tried to hang on and moor itself to a bank; but the spectacle continued to unfold, recalling a similar, bygone scene that for years had been almost forgotten. In place of that flower of the marshes, another, more human flower, seen not long since at an exhibition, returned and planted itself, revealing a variant on this dismal conception.

Then the water, that terrifying water, dried up, and in its place rose a desolate steppe, a land broken up by volcanic eruptions and ravaged by swellings and crevices, a land scorified into slag. It was as if one were visiting, on an imaginary journey using a Beer and Mädler map, one of the silent amphitheatres of the moon, the Sea of Nectar, or the Sea of Humours, or the Sea of Crises, and that, in this atmospheric void, in a cold such as one had never felt before, you were wandering in the middle of a dead, noiseless desert, terrified by the immensity of the mountain peaks that rose up all around you to vertiginous heights, their craters in the form of cups, like those of Tycho, Calippus or Eratosthenes.

And on this desolate planet there emerged from the white soil the same stalk that had just sprung from the black water; as before, buds were blooming on its metallic branches and a round pale head also swayed at the top; but its sadness was more ambiguous and melted into the irony of a dreadful smile.

* * *

Suddenly the nightmare completely broke off and a frightful waking ensued, as the inflexible face of Certainty appeared, gripping me again in her hand of iron, leading me back to life, to the waking day, to the fastidious tasks that every new morning brings.

* * *

Such were the visions evoked by an album dedicated to Goya's glory by Odilon Redon, the prince of mysterious dreams, the landscape artist of subterranean waters and of deserts convulsed by lava; by Odilon Redon the *Comprachico* Oculist of the human face, the subtle Lithographer of Suffering, the Necromancer of the Pencil, who, for the pleasure of a few aristocrats of art, has strayed into the democratic milieu of modern Paris.

THE OVERTURE TO *TANNHÄUSER*

From a landscape such as nature wouldn't know how
to create, from a landscape in which the sun pales to
the most exquisite and utmost dilution of golden
yellow, from a sublime landscape in which, under a
sickly luminous sky, the crystallised whiteness of
mountain-tops opalesce above bluish valleys; from a
landscape inaccessible to painters because it is composed solely of visual chimeras, of the silent shimmering and humid throbbing of the air, a chant
ascends, a chant singularly majestic, an august canticle springing from the souls of tired pilgrims
advancing in a group.

And this chant, with none of that female effusive-
ness, none of those wheedling prayers trying to
obtain through the perilous phoneyness of modern
worship that encounter with God reserved for the
few, swells with that certitude of pardon and a con-
viction of redemption which was borne in upon the
humble souls of the Middle Ages. Reverential and
proud, manly and honest, it tells of the appalling
fatigue of the sinner who has descended to the
depths of his conscience, the unfailing disgust of the
spiritual seer confronting the iniquities and accumulated errors in these strongholds, and it also affirms,

after a profession of faith in the redemption, the superhuman happiness of a new life, the inexpressible gladness of a reborn heart enlightened, as at Mount Thabor, by the rays of a mystic Superessence.

Then this chant grows weaker and little by little fades away; the pilgrims fan out, the sky darkens, the luminous light of day grows dim and shortly afterwards the orchestra floods this authentic and unreal scene with crepuscular gleams. It is a dissipation of colours, a fine spray of nuances, a crystalline haze of sounds which expire with the last echo of the canticle fading in the distance; and night falls on this immaterial nature, now withdrawn into itself in uneasy anticipation, created by the genius of man.

Then a cloud, irradiated with the colours of a rare flora, the expiring purples, the death-agony pinks and the moribund whites of the anenome, disperses, scattering fleecy vapours, whose ascending shades grow darker, exhaling unknown perfumes in which are mixed the biblical scent of myrrh and the voluptuously complex perfumes of modern essences.

Suddenly, in the middle of this musical scene, in this fluid and fantastical scene, the orchestra bursts out, portraying the advancing Tannhäuser in a few decisive traits, sketching him from head to foot with the outline of a heraldic melody: and the darkness is shot through with gleams; spirals of clouds take on the arched forms of haunches and palpitate with the pneumatic swelling of breasts; the blue avalanches of the heavens throng with naked forms; screams of desire, cries of lust, impulses of yearning for a carnal

Beyond leap from the orchestra, and above the undulating espalier of fainting, swooning nymphs, Venus rises, but no longer the antique Venus, the old Aphrodite, whose impeccable contours inspired lechery in gods and men during the lustful festivals of paganism, but a more profound, more terrifying Venus, a Christian Venus, if the sin against nature of coupling these two words were possible!

Indeed, this is not the unfading Beauty appointed only to earthly joys, to artistic and sensual excitations as the salacious sculptures of Greece understood it; this is the incarnation of the spirit of Evil, an effigy of omnipotent Lust, an image of the irresistible and magnificent She-Satan who is unceasingly on the lookout for Christian souls, at whom she aims her delightful and malevolent weapons.

Such has Wagner created her, this Venus, an emblem of the physical nature of the individual, an allegory of Evil struggling against Good, a symbol of our internal hell opposed to our inner heaven, leading us back in a bound through the centuries, to the impenetrable grandeur of the symbolic poem by Prudentius, that living Tannhäuser who, after years dedicated to debauchery, tore himself from the arms of the victorious She-Devil to seek refuge in the penitential adoration of the Virgin.

In fact it seems that the Venus of the musician is the descendant of the poet's Luxuria, of that pure huntress who, steeped in perfumes, crushed her victims under the force of enervating flowers; it seems that the Wagnerian Venus attracts and captivates men like the most deadly of Prudentius' deities, her

whose name the poet writes with a trembling hand:
Sodomita Libido.

But even though the idea of her recalls the allegorical entities of the Middle Ages, she brings an add-
itional spice of modernity, insinuating an intellectual
current of refinement into this molten mass of sav-
age delights; and to the naive canvas of ancient times
she adds a kind of provocative excitement, assuring
more certainly through this over-stimulation of a
nervous acuity the ultimate defeat of the hero, who
is suddenly initiated into the lascivious cerebral
complexities of the worn-out epoch in which we live
today.

And the soul of Tannhäuser buckles, his body succumbs. Deluged by ineffable promises and passionate
murmurs, he falls, delirious, into the arms of the
perverting clouds that embrace him; his melodic per-
sonality is obliterated by the triumphal hymn of
Evil. Then the tempest of roaring flesh, the lightning
flashes and electric blasts that are rumbling in the
orchestra subside; the incomparable clash of those
huge cymbals, which seems to be a transposition of
blinding purples and sumptuous golds, fades away;
and a gentle, deliciously tenuous susurration, an
almost divine rustling of adorably blue and airily
pink sounds, trembles in the nocturnal ether, which is
already beginning to brighten. Then dawn breaks,
the hesitant sky begins to whiten, as if painted with
the white sounds of the harp, and is tinged with
tentative colours which little by little become more
definite and resplendent amid a magnificent alleluia,
amid the crashing splendour of kettledrums and

brass. The sun rises, flaring out fan-like, splitting the thickening line of the horizon, climbs as if from the bottom of a lake whose watery surface seethes with her reflected rays. In the distance, the intercessionary canticle hovers, the faithful canticle of the pilgrims, cleansing the last wounds of a spirit exhausted by this diabolical struggle; and, in an apotheosis of light, in a gloriole of Redemption, Matter and Spirit soar upwards, Evil and Good are reconciled, Lust and Purity are bound together by the two musical motifs that are snaking round each other, blending the rapid, exhausting kisses of the violins, the dazzling and mournful caresses of taut, nervous strings, with the calm, majestic chorus that unfurls itself, with that mediatory melody, that canticle of the now kneeling soul celebrating its final immersion, its unshakeable constancy in the bosom of God.

And, trembling and enraptured, you come out of the vulgar hall where the miracle of this essential music has been performed, carrying with you the indelible memory of this overture to *Tannhäuser*, this prodigious and initial summary of the overwhelming grandeur of its three acts.

RESEMBLANCES

For Théodore Hannon

The hangings lifted and the strange beauties crowding behind the curtain advanced towards me, one after the other.

At first they were vague tepidities, the dying aromas of heliotrope and iris, of verbena and reseda, which imbued me with that oddly plaintive seductiveness of misty autumn skies, of the full moon's phosphoric whiteness, and of women with indistinct faces and flowing contours, with ash-blonde hair and the rosy-blue complexions of hydrangeas, women in fading iridescent skirts who came towards me, infusing everything with perfume, and then dissolved into the doleful hues of old silk and the calm, almost sleepy bouquet of old face-powders locked away for long years in the drawers of antique chests, far from the light of day.

Then this vision took flight and a subtle fragrance of bergamot and frangipane, of moss-rose and cypress, *maréchale* and new-mown hay, that had been lingering here and there, adding a flash of pink to this concert of exquisite insipidities like one of Fragonard's sensual brushstrokes, sprang up like some chic, love-struck girl with snow-dusted hair, affectionate, mischievous eyes and great flounces the colour of azure and peach-blossom; but then this too faded, little by little, and disappeared completely.

Now the *maréchale*, the new-mown hay, the heliotrope and iris, that whole palette of sensual and soothing shades, gives way to more lively tones, bolder colours, stronger odours: sandalwood, Havana cigars, magnolia, the fragrances of black and Creole women.

After these fluid brushstrokes, these misty glazes, these drowsy and tender aromas; after these feeble pinks and expiring blues, after these whip-stitched colours and tropical highlights, come shades that clamour stupidly in vulgar repetitions: the heaviness of ochres, the sluggishness of coarse greens, the dullness of browns, the dreariness of greys, and the blue-black gloominess of slate; and these are followed by heavy exhalations of seringia, of hyacinth and angel-water with their laughing, blissfully radiant faces, their banally beautiful faces, with black pomaded hair, cheeks lacquered with rouge and plastered with talc, and skirts hanging gracelessly against their fat, flabby bodies. Then come spectral apparitions, nightmare progeny, hallucinatory obsessions, emerging from wild backdrops, from backdrops of sulphuriated verdigris swimming in pistachio-green mists or in phosphorous blues, demented and cheerless beauties steeping their strange charms in the gloomy melancholy of violets, in the burning bitterness of orange, women out of Edgar Allan Poe or Baudelaire, with their tortured poses, their cruelly bitten lips, their eyelids fluttering with burning nostalgia, exalted by the superhuman joys of Gorgons, of female Titans, of extraterrestrial women, their ostentatious skirts wafting nameless perfumes, blasts of languor and passion that grip the temples, that unsettle and overthrow man's reason more easily than the fumes of Indian hemp, than the painted faces of that great modern master, Eugène Delacroix.

These evocations of another world, these wild conflagrations, these twilight tonalities, these over-stimulated emanations disappeared in their turn and a horn-blast of unthought of, incredible colours explodes.

A shimmer of purple sparks, a fanfare of scents multiplied tenfold and raised to their maximum intensity, a triumphal march, a dazzling apotheosis appears in the doorway, as of whores flaunting on their sumptuous skirts all the passion, all the magnificence, all the exaltation of reds – from the ruby-red of lacquer to the blazing fires of nasturtium, to the glorious splendours of saturn red and vermilion – and all the ostentation, all the incandescence, all the brilliance of yellows, from pale chrome to gamboge, Mars yellow, golden ochre and cadmium, all came towards me, flesh purplish and bulging, russet hair flecked with powdered gold, lips voracious, eyes gleaming, exhaling wild breaths of patchouli and amber, musk and opoponax, terrifying breaths composed of the sultriness of hot-houses, of *allegro con brios*, of shrieks and auto-da-fés, of the fiery reds and yellows of the furnace, and of conflagrations of colours and perfumes.

Then everything grew dim, and next came the primary colours: yellow, red, blue, the parent-scents of composite perfumes: tonkin musk, tuberose and amber appeared before me and united in a lengthy kiss.

As their lips touched, their colours grew weaker, their scents faded; like Phoenixes rising again from their ashes, they were going to live again in another form, in the form of secondary colours, of derivative perfumes.

Red and yellow gave way to orange; yellow and blue to green; pink and blue to purple; even the non-colours, black and white, appeared in their turn and from their entwined arms the colour grey fell heavily, a big lump of a girl that a quick kiss of blue smoothed and refined into a dreamy Cydalise: a pearl-grey hue.

And just as colours merge and are reborn anew, these essences commingled, losing their original qualities, transforming themselves, according to the vitality or the languor of their caresses, into their multifarious or rare descendants: *maréchale*, a hint of musk, amber, tuberose, cinnamon, jasmine and orange; frangipane extracted from bergamot and vanilla, from saffron and from balms of amber and musk; 'Jockey Club' born of the coupling of tuberose and orange, of Mousseline and iris, of lavender and honey.

And others . . . still others . . . shades of lilac and sulphur, of salmon and pale brown, of lacquer and cobalt green, and more . . . still more . . . *Bouquet d'Or*, Mousseline and spikenard were bursting and smoking *ad infinitum*, light, dark, delicate and heavy . . .

* * *

I awoke . . . nothing remained. Alone at the foot of my bed, Icarus, my cat, had lifted her right haunch and, with her pink tongue, was licking her ginger coat.

NOTES

*Pieces marked with an * indicate those that were added for the second edition of 1886.*

I. 'THE FOLIES-BERGÈRE IN 1879'

29 *Folies-Bergère.* The Folies-Bergère was a music-hall theatre on the Rue Richer in Paris. It was built in 1867 and was the venue for a number of spectacles such as operettas, pantomimes, concerts, and gymnastic displays. In 1880 it inaugurated a series of music concerts and in 1881 it changed its name to Concert de Paris. However, soon afterwards the Folies-Bergère re-established its old pro-gramme. The café-concert was a source of inspiration for the Impressionists, most notably for Manet and Degas – the former preferring the Folies and the latter the Café des Ambassadeurs – and both artists produced numerous paintings and prints devoted to the subject.

31 *a wooden leg and a red ribbon.* The red ribbon of the Legion of Honour was a military and civil decoration instituted by Bonaparte in 1802. The implication here is that the young man lost his leg in the Franco-Prussian war of 1870–71, in which Huysmans himself served as an infantryman before being invalided out.

32 *Ludovic de Francmesnil.* Ludovic de Vente de Francmesnil (1852–1930) was one of Huysmans' earliest friends, the two having been classmates at the Pension Hortus. They shared similar tastes in art and literature and both worked

165

in Government ministries, Huysmans at the Ministry of the Interior, Francmesnil at the Ministry of War. In the late 1870s, de Francmesnil, Léon Hennique and Paul Daniel (see below) frequently accompanied Huysmans to the Folies-Bergère.

34 *Léon Hennique.* Léon Hennique (1851–1935), a novelist and dramatist associated with the Naturalist movement. Like Huysmans, he contributed to the *Soirées de Médan* (1880) collection, and in 1881 he and Huysmans wrote a pantomime together, *Pierrot sceptique*, which was published but never performed.

34 *opoponax.* A gum resin similar to myrrh used to make a perfume with an exotic scent.

35 *Paul Daniel.* A friend of Huysmans' who worked at the Préfecture de la Seine in Paris. Huysmans, de Francmesnil and Daniel all saw the Hanlon-Lees perform, and a few years later Daniel was also among those who attended a seance held at Huysmans' flat, as recounted in Gustave Boucher's *Une Séance de Spiritisme chez J.-K. Huysmans* (1908).

37 *gouache-ing.* In the original, Huysmans coins his own word 'gouachant', derived from the opaque watercolour paint gouache. Theodore Reff notes that this reference 'points unmistakably to a pictorial influence, and precisely that of Degas, who was almost alone among the Impressionists at this time in exploiting the brilliant, matt quality of gouache.'

39 *chibouk.* A long Turkish tobacco pipe.

39 *Old Bugeaud's Cap.* A song referring to Thomas Bugeaud, a marshal of France. He joined Napoleon during the 100 days campaign, prior to the defeat at Waterloo in 1815, and distinguished himself in a battle against the Austrians at Savoy. Later, accused of repressing the rising of 1834, he became very unpopular among the people.

39 *spahi.* A member of the cavalry corps in the Ottoman Turkish army.

39 *spencer.* A short, close-fitting jacket.

39 *dances like a goat.* Maupassant used the same expression in his story 'En canot', published in *Le Bulletin Français* in 1876 and later titled 'Sur l'eau'.

39 *trois-six.* A strong alcohol that got its name because it was said that if you mixed three measures of it with three measures of water the resultant spirit was the equivalent of six measures of ordinary whisky.

40 *Marianne of Belleville.* Belleville was a quarter of Paris that was annexed in 1860 and divided between the 19th and 20th *arrondissements.* It was mainly a workers' quarter, hence the association with Marianne, the symbolic female figure who, often depicted bearing a gun and baring a breast, stood as an iconic figure of the revolutionary French Republic.

40 *Deburau.* Jean Gaspard Deburau (1796–1846), one of the most renowned pantomime artists in France. Born into a family of acrobats in Bohemia – his original name was Jan Kaspar Dvorjak – he performed with them from an early age. He joined the Théâtre des Funambules in Paris at the age of 15, where he made his name with the introduction of the figure of Pierrot, the ever-hopeful but always disappointed lover.

42 *Hanlon-Lees.* The Hanlon-Lees were a famous English mime troupe. When they made their debut in 1847 in London, the troupe consisted of John Lees, and the brothers George, William and Alfred Hanlon. However, after Lees' death in 1848, the three Hanlons were joined by their other three brothers Thomas, Edward and Frederick and their act included gymnastics and the flying trapeze. An association with the French juggler, Henri Agoust, led

the brothers to develop an act which relied more on comic and pantomimic elements. The Hanlon-Lees began performing their pantomimes, or 'fantasias of the unconscious' as Robert Storey (*French Forum*, January 1981) has called them, in Paris in 1867. Huysmans saw them a number of times and an account of the piece he describes here, called *Le Duel*, was also included in the brothers' *Mémoires et pantomimes* (1879). Huysmans saw at least two other pieces: *Pierrot menusier* and *Pierrot terrible*, and the performances of the Hanlon-Lees clearly influenced Huysmans' own attempt at a pantomime, *Pierrot sceptique*, written in collaboration with Léon Hennique. The enigmatic figure of the Pierrot recurs throughout Huysmans' work.

42 *Hogarth and Rowlandson, Gillray and Cruickshank.* English caricaturists renowned for their satirical prints and etchings. William Hogarth (1697–1764) was a painter and printmaker whose most emblematic work, contained in series such as *A Harlot's Progress* and *A Rake's Progress*, exposed the corruption and hypocrisy of fashionable society. James Gillray (1757–1815) and Thomas Rowlandson (1756–1827) were the two great caricaturists of the Georgian period, the fathers of the political cartoon. George Cruickshank (1792–1878) was one of the most prolific comic illustrators of the time. Aside from his own comic books, he provided illustrations for Walter Scott's *Waverly Novels* and Dickens' *Sketches by Boz* and *Oliver Twist*.

43 *Robert le Diable.* A popular and enormously influential opera by Meyerbeer which was first performed at the Paris Opera in 1831. It has been described as the first Romantic opera of the 19th century.

44 *fake Louvois fountains.* The original Fontaine de Louvois was erected in 1839 by Louis Vincent.It is located in the Square Louvois, in the 2nd *arrondissement*.

44 *Alhambresque*. The citadel of Alhambra, at the base of the Sierra Nevada in Spain, was the ancient residence of the kings of Granada. It is one of the best-known examples of medieval Islamic architecture in Europe. There was also a music hall on the Faubourg-du-Temple called the Alhambra.

44 *Poyet*. The original has 'Poret', but there is no trace of an architect by that name, so it is possible this is a misprint for 'Poyet'. Bernard Poyet (1742–1829) was the architect charged with carrying out Carmontelle's plan for the redevelopment of the Parc Monceau. Carmontelle envisioned a space that would 'bring all eras and all countries together in a single garden'. The Parc was arranged as a series of architectural tableaux and included a windmill, a watermill, a minaret, an obelisque, a pyramid, a temple, Turkish tents and so on.

44 *Duval*. Charles Duval (1800–1876) was an architect renowned for his picturesque, oriental-style buildings. His works in Paris included the Bataclan, a café-concert in the style of a Chinese pagoda which was built in 1864–65 and was the venue for ballets and concerts, the Grand Café, the Delta Café, the Eldorado and the Alcazar.

II. 'THE DANCEHALL AT *THE BRASSERIE EUROPÉENNE* IN GRENELLE'*

45 *Grenelle*. A commune of Paris, now forming part of the 15th *arrondissement*. Formerly an industrial quarter, its proximity to the École Militaire and the Champ de Mars accounts for its association with the military.

48 *cavalier seul*. A dance move in the quadrille in which the gentleman advances on his own.

49 *Gros-Caillou*. A residential quarter in the 7th *arrondissement*, extending from the Seine to the Avenue de La

Motte-Piquet and across the Champ-de-Mars. It took its
name from a large rock (*caillou*) marking its border
which was destroyed in 1738, and the appellation
stuck despite also being used as the name of a popular
brothel. In 1877, Huysmans began writing a novel, provi-
sionally entitled *Gros-Caillou*, but it was subsequently
abandoned. An earlier version of this piece, which originally formed the first chapter of the novel, appeared
in *La Gaulois* in 1880 under the title 'Tabatières et
Riz-Pain-Sel'.

53 *cuirassier*. A cavalry soldier in the French army wearing a
cuirass, a piece of body armour comprising a breastplate
and a backplate joined together.

55 *Cail et Cie*. Founded by Jean-François Cail (1804–1871),
Cail et Cie was one of the largest and most important
engineering works in Paris.

56 *the Salon de Mars and the Ardoise*. In the earlier version of
this story, 'Tabatières et Riz-Pain-Sel', mentioned above,
Huysmans describes the Ardoise as a low dancehall, and
the Salon de Mars as a public house in the suburbs.

56 *Commissariat*. The Commissariat or *intendance militaire*,
was the branch of the military service which dealt with its
practical and administrative needs. It included quartermasters and administrative clerks.

60 *Heaps of saucers*. Parisian waiters used to calculate the
amount that had been drunk by the number of saucers left
on the table.

62 *If you're hungry*. An old French saying that relies on rhyme
for its effect: *Si t'as faim, mange ton poing* [or '*main*'], *et
garde l'autre pour demain* [Literally: If you're hungry eat
your fist, and keep the other for tomorrow]. There doesn't
seem to be an equivalent for drinking, which is perhaps
why Madame Tampois can't remember it.

65 *Avenue de Lowendal.* An avenue in the 15th *arrondissement*, running from the Place Cambron in Grenelle to Les Invalides, on which the École Militaire is situated.

III. PARISIAN CHARACTERS

'The Bus Conductor'

First published in *La Cravache*, 19th November 1876.

70 *Danaide-like task.* In Greek mythology, Danaus was forced against his will to marry his fifty daughters to the fifty sons of Aegyptus. He ordered them to stab their husbands on their wedding night, which they all did except Hypermnestra. After their deaths, the Danaides were punished in the underworld by having to perpetually fill leaking jars with water.

71 *Machut.* Character in a popular one-act farce by Eugène Labiche, *La Grammaire* (1867). Machut is the father of five children, 'with another one on the way'.

71 *Numbers 8, 9, 10, get on.* Formerly, those queuing for a bus had to take numbered tickets and if the bus was crowded the conductor would call out the numbers of those allowed on.

'The Streetwalker'

73 *apéritif.* In the original Huysmans uses the word '*apéritive*', a newly-coined slang word which by the 1880s had entered common usage. Alfred Delvau, in his *Dictionnaire de la Langue Verte* (1889), defines *l'apérative* as 'a woman of easy virtue who was to the high-class hooker what the chrysalis is to the butterfly'. She got her name from the way in which she frequented fashionable cafés looking for

men to buy her an 'apéritif' as a prelude to a more intimate physical exchange.

73 *picolo*. A perjorative term for cheap, locally-made red wine.

73 *bichloride of mercury*. Commonly used in the treatment of syphilis before the discovery of antibiotics.

73 *Polyte*. A contraction of Hippolyte [Hippolytus]. Huysmans is making an ironic allusion to the Greek myth, in which Phaedre falls in love with Hippolytus and dies after he rejects her advances.

75 *Rigolboche*. A drink presumably named after Amélie Marguerite Badel, known popularly as Rigolboche, the dancer who invented the can-can. Her autobiography, *Mémoires de Rigolboche*, appeared in 1860.

76 *vice-squad threatens*. In the original Huysmans uses the word *brême*, a slang word which was used to denote the act of being inscribed by the *police des moeurs* (vice squad) onto a register of public prostitutes. Once a prostitute was registered she had to undergo regular medical examinations and if found to be diseased would be sent to the Lourcine hospital (see below) for treatment.

76 *Lourcine*. An asylum for women with venereal disease (now the Broca hospital). A collection of 442 plaster casts of syphilitics taken from patients at the Lourcine is held in the Musée de Moulages at the Saint-Louis hospital in Paris.

'The Washerwoman'

77 *Nausicaa*. In Homer's *Odyssey*, Nausicaa is the Phoenician princess who meets the shipwrecked Odysseus when she comes down to the sea-shore to wash her clothes.

77 *of Homeric and tedious memory*. In Huysmans' novel *En Ménage* (1881), André Jayant, recalling his school days,

complains about having to read 'Homer's stupefying nonsense'.

77 *mi-carême*. During the nineteenth century there was a tradition in Paris during the mid-Lenten feast (*mi-carême*) of holding a carnival-like parade of 'Queens', in which a Queen of Washerwomen (*Reine des Blanchisseuses*) would be chosen.

77 *Lancret*. Nicolas Lancret (1690–1743), a genre painter famous for his rural scenes of fêtes and gatherings, such as *Fête in a Wood* and *Girls Bathing*.

77 *true profession being no doubt more lucrative, if less mentionable*. A survey carried out between 1878–1887 by Dr. O. Commenge and published as *La Prostitution Clandestine à Paris* (1897) found that among the common female professions, laundering had one of the highest incidences of clandestine prostitution.

78 *Rue aux Ours*. An old street in the 3rd *arrondissement* of Paris, near Les Halles.

78 *battledores*. A wooden instrument like a paddle, used in washing.

78 *canezous*. Light muslin smocks or jackets. According to Victor Hugo in *Les Misérables*, the *canezou* was a kind of muslin spencer, invented in Marseilles, its name being 'a corruption of the words *quinze août* [15th of August], pronounced after the fashion of the Canebière, signifying fine weather, heat, and midday.'

'The Journeyman Baker'

First published in *La Cravache*, 17th December 1876.

80 *Watteau*. Jean-Antoine Watteau (1684–1721). Influenced by Rubens, Veronese and Titian, Watteau was one of the

leading painters of the early 18th century. His work had a huge impact on subsequent landscape and genre painting.

80 *Cydalises*. A character in Balzac's *La Cousine Bette*, Cydalise was a magnificent looking woman from Valognes, Normandy, who went to Paris in 1840 to make money out of her beauty.

80 *Gilles*. One of Watteau's most enigmatic and emblematic paintings, also known as *Pierrot*, is a full-length portrait of Gilles, a stock figure in Italian comedy dressed in a white clown's costume. The picture is in the Louvre, so Huysmans would undoubtedly have seen it numerous times during his frequent visits to the gallery.

'The Chestnut-seller'

First published in *La Cravache*, 3rd December 1876.

85 *gatherings of the mob in front of pharmacies*. At times of civil unrest, pharmacies were subject to looting by the mob in order to get the ingredients for making gun-powder.

'The Barber'*

First published in *La Vie Moderne*, 19th February 1881.

88 *currycombs*. Metal combs used to groom a horse.

90 *Eau de Lubin*. A citrus-scented *eau-de-toilette* formulated by Pierre-François Lubin in 1798.

IV. LANDSCAPES

'The Bièvre'

First published in *La République des Lettres*, February 1877.

93 *Henry Céard.* It was Henry Céard (1851–1924) who first introduced Huysmans to Emile Zola in 1876. Céard, like Ludovic de Francmesnil, worked at the Ministry of War, but he was also a writer. A member of the Naturalist group, he contributed the story, 'La Saignée', to the *Soirées de Médan* collection.

93 *Bièvre.* The Bièvre, Paris's 'second' river, ran from Saint-Cyr, south of Versailles, through the Gobelins, before joining the Seine near the Gare d'Austerlitz. The water from the Bièvre was vital to the expansion and development of the Gobelins tapestry factory in the seventeenth and eighteenth centuries. By the nineteenth century the river was used by 24 tanneries and numerous other industrial manufacturers, though closer to Paris itself its waters were increasingly hemmed in by slum housing. In his essay, 'A river runs through it: la Bièvre, Huysmans and nineteenth-century Paris', Leonard Koos describes how the Bièvre was 'replenished on a daily basis with all types of human refuse and waste, soapy and bleach-filled laundry run-off, chemical dyes, and animal carcasses . . .' Parts of the river began to be covered over from about 1828 and much of what remained was paved over during the redevelopments carried out by Baron Haussmann. Huysmans had a life-long fascination with the Bièvre river: his first book, *Le Drageoir à épices* (1874), included a section on the Bièvre and its environs, and in 1886 he published his definitive account of the river in an Amsterdam review, *De Nieuwe Gids*, which later appeared in book form in 1890.

93 *destruction of its gullies and its trees.* This was written during the latter period of the Haussmannisation of Paris.

Huysmans deplored the fact that many of the sights and locations of his youth, especially those in and around the Latin quarter, had been destroyed by the construction of Haussmann's impersonal *grands boulevards*.

93 *Rue du Pot-au-Lait and the Chemin de la Fontaine-à-Mulard*. Two roads close to the Bièvre river which no longer exist. Huysmans would have been familiar with them from his regular walks through the area.

94 *artesian well at the Butte aux Cailles*. The Butte aux Cailles, a natural, 63-meter-high hill overlooking Paris, situated near today's Rue Vergniaud and the Rue de Tolbiac, was one of the last revolutionary strongholds of the Paris Commune in 1871. In 1866 work began on drilling a six-and-a-half-foot artesian well into the Butte in order to provide more water for the city.

96 *intimists*. Artists whose subject matter is the personal, non-public side of life, such as the Flemish and Dutch genre painters of the 17th century.

'The Poplar Inn'

99 *barrière Blanche*. A route out of Paris, along the Route de Fontainebleau.

99 *Bicêtre*. A large hospital situated on a hillside overlooking the Bièvre, a short distance from Paris. Many of its inmates were mental patients.

100 *Buc*. A town on the Bièvre, to the south of Versailles.

'The Rue de la Chine'

101 *Jules Bobin*. Jean-Jules-Athanase Bobin (1834–1905), known to his friends as 'le Professeur' because of his

pedantic air and great erudition, was a friend of Huysmans. A colleague of Henry Céard and Ludovic de Francmesnil at the Ministry of War, Bobin was a bibliophile with a taste for, among other things, the exotic, the erotic and the occult. Céard relates how Bobin used to bring rare works to Huysmans' flat to read out loud.

101 *Ménilmontant.* One of the *quartiers* in Paris' 20th *arrondissement*. In the Second Empire the area was mainly inhabited by workers and craftsmen.

102 *Gobelins.* A district to the south of Paris that got its name from the Reims dyer Jean Gobelin, who established his tapestry workshop by the Bièvre river in 1450. In 1662, the Gobelins maufactory was taken over on behalf of the crown and during the seventeenth and eighteenth centuries the elaborate tapestries that were produced were among the finest in Europe, and renowned for their depiction of scenes from mythology, classical literature and the Bible. Production was severely hit by the Revolution, and during the Second Empire the weavers were reduced to copying paintings and the area's decline continued until the end of the nineteenth century.

103 *Tenon hospital.* A Parisian hospital situated on the Rue de la Chine in the 20th *arrondissement*, named after the surgeon Jacques Tenon (1724–1816). It was built between 1870 and 1878.

'*View from the ramparts of north Paris*'

107 *Parcs-Monceau.* The *Parc-Monceau* in the 17th *arrondissement* originally formed part of the grounds belonging to Philippe Egalité. The park was constructed in 1778 and decorated with numerous 'follies': Chinese bridges, windmills, obelisks and ruined temples, as well as a boating lake. It became a public park in 1794, after the Revolution.

V. FANTASIES AND FORGOTTEN CORNERS

'The Tallow candle: a prose ballad'

First published in *Musée des Deux Mondes*, 15th May 1876.

111 *Gabriel Thyébaut* (1854–1915). A close friend of Huysmans who worked at the Préfecture de la Seine in Paris.

111 *Carcel lamp.* A large mechanical lamp in which the oil is pumped to the wick tube by clockwork. It was named after its inventor, the French clockmaker Bertrand Guillaume Carcel (1750–1812).

112 *Gerrit Dou.* A Dutch painter from Leiden, Gerrit Dou (1613–1675) was known chiefly as the head of the 'Precise' school. He was Rembrandt's pupil from 1628 to 1631, but after he left Rembrandt, he developed his own style. Some of his best known works, such as *Astronomer by Candlelight* (1655), *The Evening School* (circa 1660) and *Old Woman with a Candle* (1661), show his skill at handling artificial light effects.

112 *Godfried Schalcken.* Born at Dordrecht, Godfried Schalcken (1643–1706) studied under Samuel van Hoogstraten before moving to Leiden, where he became Gerrit Dou's pupil in the early 1660s. Like Dou, he was particularly admired for his mastery in reproducing the effect of candlelight, such as in his portrait *Girl Threading a Needle by Candlelight* (circa 1670).

*'Damiens'**

113 *Robert Caze.* The poet, journalist and novelist, Robert Caze (1853–1886) had something of a stormy life. He agitated against Napoleon III and took an active part in the Commune, after which he had to live in exile for a period. On his return to Paris after the amnesty of 1880, he not only

attended Goncourt's *grenier*, but also held his own *soirées* at 13, Rue Condorcet, where Huysmans and Hennique met some of the leading Impressionist painters. Caze was wounded in a duel with Charles Viguier on 15 February 1886 and died six weeks afterwards. Huysmans and Edmond de Goncourt visited him on his death bed. After Caze's death his widow sold sixty of Huysmans' letters to her husband to a dealer. On learning of the sale, Huysmans immediately purchased back the letters and destroyed them, fearing that their indecent contents might compromise him.

114 *Rue Bonaparte.* A street in Saint-Germain-des-Prés well-known for its bookshops and antique dealers.

115 *Damiens.* Robert François Damiens (1715–1757), the son of a farming family in Arras, attempted to assassinate Louis XV on 5 January 1757 with a pen-knife. The King was barely wounded, but Damiens was subjected to brutal tortures, only some of which Huysmans mentions. The hand that held the knife was put into a fire, and boiling lead, oil and pitch poured onto his body. He was then quartered, the traditional punishment for regicides, by being pulled apart by horses, and his limbs subsequently burnt and the ashes scattered. Michel Foucault makes the torture of Damiens the cornerstone of his critique of crime, criminality and the State in *Discipline and Punish: the Birth of the Prison* (1977).

115 *Place de Grève.* The traditional site of public executions in Paris. A guillotine was set up there during the French Revolution. The last execution took place there in 1830 and it is now the Place de l'Hôtel de Ville.

'Roast meat: a prose poem'

117 *Alexis Orsat.* Louis-Alexis Orsat (1837–1906), a friend of Huysmans' who worked at the Ministry of War. They

regularly lunched together at an old-fashioned restaurant on the Rue de Grenelle.

117 *Seltzer water.* A carbonated, highly effervescent mineral water from Seltz in Germany that was thought to have medicinal properties.

'A Café'

121 *café with an unchanging clientele.* The café Huysmans describes was most likely the Café des Oiseaux, 12 Place d'Anvers, at the corner of the Square d'Anvers and Rue de Dunkerque, near the Gare du Nord. The glass cases of birds have long since been removed.

124 *Bar-le-Duc.* An ancient town in the Meuse, where there was indeed a small bistrot-tabac, called the Bar des Oiseaux, containing stuffed birds.

'Ritornello'

First published in *Le Drageoir à épices* (1874).

125 *Get it here! Get it here!* In the original, Huysmans uses the words '*il arrive! il arrive*', probably part of an old Paris street cry used by fishmongers. Louis Sébastien Mercier (1740–1814) recorded the full cry in his *Tableaux de Paris* (1781–1788) as '*Voilà le maquereau* [mackerel] *qui n'est pas mort; il arrive, il arrive!*'

'The Armpit'

126 *Guy de Maupassant.* One of the best, and best known, short story writers of the 19th century, Guy de Maupassant (1850–1893) produced almost 300 stories, six novels and

three travel books in his short life. Like Huysmans, Maupassant was a civil servant, working first at the Ministry of Maritime Affairs and then at the Ministry of Education. He was one of the original members of the *groupe de Médan*, and contributed his story 'Boule-de-suif', which Huysmans called 'the pearl of the volume', to the *Soirées de Médan* (1880). Maupassant contracted syphilis in his early 20s and the disease affected his mind towards the end of his life; he tried to cut his own throat in 1892 and was committed to an asylum where he died the following year.

*'Low tide'**

129   *Rue Legendre, in the Batignolles.* A street named after Louis Legendre, a revolutionary politician who took part in the storming of the Bastille. The Batignolles district is one of the *quartiers* in the 17th *arrondissement*, bounded to the north by an important railway depot and goods yard, and to the south by the Gare St.-Lazare. The Batignolles became an important centre of Impressionist activity. Those gathering to meet at the Café Guerbois, near the Place de Clichy, especially on Thursdays, included Manet, Degas, Sisley and Renoir as well as critics such as Edmond Duranty and Théodore Duret. The riverside suburb of Argenteuil, the subject of a number of Impressionist paintings, could be reached from the Gare St.-Lazare in just 15 minutes.

129   *percaline.* A glazed calico used, among other things, on tailor's dummies.

130   *Curtius Museum.* Constructed in the early 17th century by a local arms manufacturer, Jean Curtius, this renowned museum in Liège, Belgium, contains a wealth of collections that span the Frankish eras, the Middle Ages and the 18th century. Its collection includes important pieces such as the stone sculpture, *La Vierge de Dom Rupert*, and Bishop Notger's *Evangelistary*, from around the year 900.

'Obsession'*

First published in *Revue Moderniste*, 30 October 1885.

132 *Edmond de Goncourt.* Edmond de Goncourt (1822–1896), together with his younger brother Jules, wrote a series of novels, including *Germinie Lacertaux* (1864), *Manette Salomon* (1867) and *Madame Gervaisais* (1869), which had a huge influence on the shape and form of the realist novel in France during the latter half of the 19th century. Huysmans always acknowledged his debt to Goncourt as a writer and it would be true to say that, in terms of style at least, Huysmans was more a disciple of Goncourt's than he was of Zola's. Their somewhat uneasy friendship began when Huysmans sent the older writer a copy of his first novel, *Marthe, histoire d'une fille*, in 1876. Huysmans was, for a time, a regular if reluctant guest at the famous Goncourt *grenier*, the monthly gathering of writers and artists at Goncourt's sumptuously decorated house in Auteuil. In the late 1880s, Goncourt added Huysmans to his list of future academicians, and in 1903, when the Académie Goncourt was finally inaugurated, Huysmans, as its oldest member became the *ipso facto* President.

132 *Paul Ychinel, le père Spicase, Astre à Caen, lady Scorde, miss Tigry.* A series of puns of the kind found in cryptic crossword clues. The answers are 'Pulchinel' (Punchinello), 'perspicace' (perspicacious), 'astrakan' (astrakhan), 'les discordes' (misunderstandings), 'mistigris' (Jack of Clubs).

132 *the Oedipuses of the Café du Grand-Balcon.* A cryptic reference to the solvers of crossword puzzles (Oedipus solved the riddle of the Sphinx). The Café du Grand-Balcon was situated near the Porte Saint-Denis in Paris.

133 *journeys made trying to raise money.* After the death of his mother in 1876, Huysmans took over the responsibility of running a book bindery that had originally been bought by

his step-father, who died in 1867. By the early 1880s, the bindery was in serious financial difficulties, with bankruptcy a real possibility, and, as a consequence, the loss of his job in the Civil Service. In a letter to Gabriel Thyébaut in August 1887, Huysmans wrote that the bindery was dragging him into a 'rat-trap of difficulties' and that he was having to arrange a 'whole heap of meetings to try and find work and money'.

134 *all the odium, all the contempt with which I've been showered.* The attacks made on Huysmans following the publication of *A Rebours* (1884) were probably still fresh in his mind when he wrote this piece. In a letter to Zola on 25th May 1884, Huysmans explained that the book had roused anger on all sides: 'I've trodden on everyone's toes; the Catholics are exasperated, others accuse me of being a cleric in disguise ... the Romantics are outraged by its attacks on Hugo, Gautier and Leconte de Lisle, and the Naturalists by its contempt for modern life.' In a *Preface* written twenty years after the book, Huysmans recalled how reviewers had treated him as a 'misanthropic impressionist', and suggested he would benefit from a course of cold showers. He was also ridiculed in public by the influential drama critic, Francisque Sarcey who said 'he'd be hanged if he could understand a single word of the book'.

VI. STILL LIFES

'The Herring'

First published under the title 'Le Hereng Saur' in *Le Drageoir à épices* (1874).

139 *Alfred Alavoine.* The Alavoines were friends of Huysmans' parents and were listed as witnesses on Huysmans' birth certificate. Alfred Alavoine was presumably their son.

139 *Judea bitumen, etc.* Huysmans here shows his knowledge of the artist's craft, listing the names of various pigments and materials that a painter might use: Judea bitumen was a black etching ground, for example, while Cassel earth is a dark brown pigment.

139 *Scheele's green.* A green pigment, consisting of an hydrous arsenite of copper, named after the Swedish chemist, Karl Wilhelm Scheele (1742–1786).

139 *Van Dyck brown.* A very dark brown pigment made from peat.

139 *orpiments.* A golden coloured pigment used in painting since antiquity.

139 *Sumach ochre.* A yellow dye extracted from the sumach plant.

139 *Mars yellow.* A pigment made from iron oxide that goes back to the 17th century.

'The Epinal Print'

First published in *Musée des Deux Mondes*, 15th April 1875.

140 *Epinal print.* Distinctive coloured prints depicting a variety of scenes in realistic but stereotypical manner which were produced in the French town of Epinal in the early nineteenth century. The prints became so popular that the term 'image d'Epinal' is now used to refer to any form of stereotypical representation. The print Huysmans describes is almost certainly a lithograph by Charles Pinot, entitled *Juif Errant*, which was printed sometime after 1872.

140 *Eugène Monstrosier.* The proprietor of *Le Musée des Deux-Mondes*, a paper in which Huysmans published a number

of his early prose pieces including an earlier version of 'The Epinal Print'.

141 *Artaxerxes*. King of Persia whose generosity to the Jews is recorded in the Old Testament Book of Ezra.

142 *Wandering Jew*. The legend of the Wandering Jew goes back to the Middle Ages. It was popularly believed that he was a man who had offended Jesus on his way to the crucifixion, and had been cursed by him to walk the earth alone until the end of the world.

142 *Isaac Laquedem*. The name given in Flanders to the Wandering Jew. Huysmans may have been familiar with Alexandre Dumas' unfinished poem of the same name, but it is probably no coincidence that in April of 1875, the same month 'The Epinal Print' was published, 30,000 Parisians followed the funeral cortege of Edgar Quinet, the poet of *Ahasverus* (1874), another name by which the Wandering Jew was known.

143 *gamboge*. A gum-resin used as a pigment giving a bright yellow colour.

VII. PARAPHRASES

*'Nightmare'**

First published in *La Revue Indépendante*, in February 1885, under the title 'Le nouvel Album d'Odilon Redon'.

149 *Sennacherib*. King of Assyria (705–681 BC), who spend much of his reign fighting to keep lands won in battle by his father. He laid siege to Jerusalem (circa 701 BC), captured and destroyed Babylon (circa 690 BC), and built a lavish palace at Nineveh.

151 *the Dhuis and the Vanne*. Two massive aqueducts that

provide Paris with water. The Vanne aqueduct is 136 km long and feeds the Montsouris reservoir, while the Dhuis, to the south-east of Paris, stretches to 131 km.

152 *infusoria, flagellates, monera, protoplasms*. Huysmans' suggestion that Redon's images were inspired by microscopic organisms caused a certain amount of friction between the two men. In his autobiography, *A Soi-même* (1922), Redon denied that he used microscopes or other optical devices to produce his fantastical visions.

152 *Bathybius*. T. H. Huxley's name for a gelatinous substance found at the bottom of the ocean consisting of a formless mass of protoplasm and thought by him to be the simplest form of life. Later research indicated that it was in fact an inorganic precipitate.

153 *scorified*. Reduced to dross or slag by the action of intense heat.

153 *Beer and Mädler*. Two German astronomers, Wilhelm Beer (1797–1850), an amateur observer, and Johann Heinrich Mädler (1794–1874), a professional, worked for four years to produce their *Mappa selenographica* (1834–37), a large-scale and richly detailed map of the moon, which was perhaps the most influential lunar publication of the century.

154 *Goya's glory*. Odilon Redon's set of six lithographs inspired by the work of Francesco Goya (1746–1828), *Hommage à Goya*, was published in Paris by Lemercier et Cie in 1885 in a limited edition of 50. Huysmans follows the series of lithographs quite closely, but with a number of interesting changes and omissions. The plates Huysmans describes are as follows: Plate I. *Dans mon rêve, je vis au Ciel un VIS-AGE DE MYSTÈRE* (In my dream, I saw a FACE OF MYSTERY in the Sky); Plate II. *La FLEUR du MARECAGE, une tête humaine et triste* (The MARSH FLOWER, a sad, human head); Plate IV. *Il y eut aussi des ETRES EMBRYONNAIRES* (There were also

EMBRYONIC BEINGS); Plate V. *Un étrange JONGLEUR* (A strange JUGGLER); and Plate VI. *Au réveil j'aperçus la DÉESSE de l'INTELLIGIBLE, au profil sévère et dur* (On awaking I saw the severe and stern profile of the GODDESS of the INTELLIGIBLE). Huysmans' misses out Plate III altogether, perhaps because he felt it didn't match the others in the series, and his description of the smiling flower is possibly a description of a variant of Plate II, such as the *Marsh Flower* of 1885, or a composite drawn from Redon's other pictures.

154 *Odilon Redon*. Huysmans first came across the work of Odilon Redon (1840–1916) during the latter's first exhibition at the premises of the Parisian weekly review *La Vie Moderne*, in 1881. The show, which was comprised of charcoal sketches, attracted almost no critical attention, though Huysmans singled it out in a note at the end of his review of the Salon of 1881 and included a fuller account in the Appendix to *L'Art Moderne* (1883). They became close friends soon afterwards before drifting apart in the 1890s.

154 *landscape artist of subterranean waters*. In June 1886, Huysmans and Arij Prins visited the sewers and the catacombes of Paris. In a letter to Gabriel Thyébaut a few days later, Huysmans described these underground landscapes as 'Redoniformes'.

154 *Comprachico*. Huysmans probably came across the term comprachicos in Victor Hugo's *L'Homme qui rit* (The Man Who Laughs), which was published in 1869. The *comprachicos*, from the Spanish meaning 'child-buyer', were a group of strange, seventeenth century vagrants who kidnapped children, deformed or mutilated them and then sold them as exhibits for travelling freak-shows. The reference to Redon being an 'oculist' alludes to the fact that the human eye, often in strange or distorted form, is a recurring element in Redon's work.

'The Overture to Tannhaüser'*

First published in the *Revue Wagnerienne*, 8th April 1885. When Edouard Dujardin, the founder of the *Revue Wagnerienne*, asked Huysmans to write something for his paper, Huysmans replied that he had no objections, but that he'd never heard a note of Wagner. Dujardin provided tickets for Huysmans and Stephane Mallarmé to attend a performance of the *Overture* at the Théâtre du Château d'Eau on 3 April 1885. Huysmans based his piece around Wagner's own description of the *Overture*, which was included in the original programme notes.

156 *Mount Thabor*. A mountain situated in Galilee, which has been the object of numerous spiritual comparisons in the Bible and was traditionally thought to be the scene of the Transfiguration.

157 *Prudentius*. Aurelius Clemens Prudentius (348–circa 410) a Christian poet born in Northern Spain. Of noble birth, he received a liberal education and practised law, though from 392 he spent much of his time writing poems on Christian themes. At the age of 57 he renounced the vanities of the world and retired to a monastery, where he died soon afterwards. His works include the *Peristephanon*, the *Libri contra Symmachum* and the *Psychomachia* [The Battle of the Soul], the latter being one of the most widely read books of the middle ages and a huge influence on the iconography of medieval art.

157 *Luxuria*. In Prudentius's *Psychomachia*, an extended allegory in which a succession of Christian virtues battle with corresponding pagan vices: Pudicitia (Chastity) defeats Sodomita Libido (Sodomitical lust), for example, and Sobrietas (Sobriety) defeats Luxuria (Self-indulgence). Prudentius also describes Luxuria winning her battles over the other Virtues by scattering flowers about her, their fatally sweet scent 'unmanning' her adversaries and crushing their strength.

'Resemblances'

First published in *La République des Lettres*, 6th August 1876.

160 *Théodore Hannon*. The Belgian painter, poet and journalist
Théodore Hannon (1851–1916) became the editor of the
Brussels' paper, *L'Artiste* in 1877. Hannon turned the
paper into an organ for the nascent Naturalist movement,
publishing work by Zola, Huysmans, Henry Céard and
Léon Hennique. It was in *L'Artiste* that an earlier version
of 'Resemblances' was reprinted in 1877, and in which
Huysmans' short story 'Sac au dos' was first published in
1878. Huysmans met Hannon in 1876 when he was in
Brussels looking for a publisher for his first novel. The two
men spent several evenings in the brothels of the Rue
Saint-Laurent and in an article published later that year
Huysmans wrote that Brussels wasn't the staid city he had
thought, but rather 'the Promised Land of strong beer and
whores, the Canaan of drink and debauchery'. In 1881,
Huysmans wrote a laudatory preface to Hannon's book of
poems *Rimes de joie*, comparing him with Charles
Baudelaire, but the poet ended their friendship a couple of
years later, and when the book was reprinted he omitted
Huysmans' preface.

160 *verbena*. A small, perennial herb with tiny purple flowers.
It can be used medically to treat colds and coughs, as well
as liver and indigestion problems.

160 *reseda*. A perennial plant with allegedly calming medicinal
properties. Its flowers are greenish white with yellow or
orange highlights.

160 *Fragonard*. Jean-Honoré Fragonard (1732–1806), a French
painter whose work embodied the rococo spirit. Huysmans'
description brings to mind the pink skinned female
revellers in Fragonard's *The Bathers* (1865), a picture that
he would have been familiar with, as it hangs in the
Louvre.

161 *Edgar Allan Poe or Baudelaire.* Charles Baudelaire (1821–1867) was instrumental in introducing the work of Edgar Allan Poe (1809–1849) to France, mainly through his translations of the American's stories, two collections of which were published in 1856 and 1857. One of the features of Poe's work, such as in the poem 'Annabel Lee' and in the story 'The Fall of the House of Usher', was the chilling elision of youthful female beauty and the spectre of death. Baudelaire saw Poe as a kindred spirit and his work, too, is characterised by an obsession with beauty, corruption and death.

162 *female Titans.* The six daughters of Ouranos and Gaia, the Titanides, were the female counterparts of the Titans.

162 *Eugène Delacroix.* Eugène Delacroix (1798–1863) was the leading romantic painter in 19th century France. His most iconic painting was *Liberty Leading the People* (1830), but he was also renowned for his canvases inspired by oriental subjects, such as *The Massacre of Chios* (1824) and *The Death of Sardanapalus* (1827).

163 *Cydalise.* See note to 'The Journeyman Baker'.

163 *Jockey Club.* An after-shave cologne for gentlemen, produced in America in 1840.

163 *Mousseline.* A moss rose with a sweet fragrance, also known as Aldred de Dalmas, introduced by Portemer in 1855.

163 *Bouquet d'Or.* A rose introduced by Jean-Claude Ducher in 1872 with a complex, fruity scent.

Books by J.-K. Huysmans available from Dedalus:

The Cathedral

En Route

La-Bas

The Oblate of St Benedict

Parisian Sketches

Là-Bas – *J.-K. Huysmans*

"Huysmans' dark masterpiece, published in the same year as *The Picture of Dorian Gray*, is a serious, uncompromisingly learned depiction of Hell through which the search for spiritual meaning must lead. The protagonist, Durtal, is investigating the life of Gilles de Rais, mass-murderer and unlikely – or not so unlikely – companion-in-arms of Joan of Arc. Long meditation on the nature of art, guilt, the satanic and the divine take him to a black mass. This superb new translation by Brendan King vividly recalls the allusive, proto-expressionist vigour of the original; images snarl and spring at the reader. A fine introduction shows where Huysmans's mystical quest ended, and the notes prove vital."

Murrough O'Brien in *The Independent on Sunday*

"Huysmans' novel, though it is clearly rooted in the preoccupations of the late 19th century, is remarkably prophetic about the concerns of our own recent *fin de siecle*. With its allusions to, amongst other things, Satanic child abuse, alternative medicine, New Age philosophy and female sexuality, the novel has clearly a lot to say to a contemporary audience. As with most of Huysmans' books, the pleasure in reading is not necessarily from its overarching plot-line, but in set pieces, such as the extraordinary sequences in which Gilles de Rais wanders through a wood that suddenly metamorphoses into a series of copulating organic forms, the justly famous word-painting of Matthias Grunewald's *Crucifixion* altarpiece, or the brutally erotic scenes, crackling with sexual tension, between Durtal and Madame Chantelouve. If it is about anything, *La-Bas* is about Good and Evil. This enlightening new translation will be especially useful to students of literature. Not only does it contain an introduction that puts Huysmans in context for those who are new to his work, it also includes extensive notes to unlock the mass of obscure words that litter the text, and references to a vast array of scientists, false messiahs and misfits whose ideas went into the concoction of this strangely fascinating book."

Beryl Bainbridge in *The Spectator*

£7.99   ISBN 1 873982 74 7   329p   B.Format

The Cathedral – *J.-K. Huysmans*

"Durtal extols the flaming raptures of the mystical Gothic, tries to comprehend the stone text of Chartres and is extremely funny about the horrors of living in the provinces, although equally viperish on the subject of Parisian literary life. These books mark a 19th century spiritual journey undertaken by a very modern sensibility; Durtal's wicked, witty, self-lacerating voice could be that of a contemporary medieval scholar with a bad case of mystical anomie."

Elizabeth Young in *City Limits*

"A wonderful picture of the inner meaning of Gothic architecture."

The Daily Telegraph

"Although the main character in *The Cathedral* is Durtal, the cathedral is the main focus of the book. Durtal's spiritual awakening is explored through his homage to, and desire to unravel the meaning of, Chartres Cathedral. Crafted with painstaking attention to detail, the novel is both an account of a conversion and a detailed examination of the language of medieval art. So thorough is Huysmans' description of the cathedral that the book has even been sold as a guide to the building."

Dr Penelope Woolf

£7.99   ISBN 1 873982 62 3   339p   B.Format

En Route – *J.-K. Huysmans*

"*En Route* continues the story of Durtal, a modern anti-hero; solitary, agonised and alienated. Robbed of religion and plunged into decadence by the pressures of modern life, Durtal discovers a new road to Rome. Art, architecture and music light his way back to God. For Durtal, God's death is a temporary demise, and by the end of the novel, he is morally mended and spiritually healed."

David Blow

£7.99   ISBN 1 873982 14 3   313p   B.Format

The Oblate of St Benedict – *J.-K. Huysmans*

The final part of Huysmans' alter ego, Durtal's, spiritual journey. From the satanism of *La-Bas* (1891) he makes his way to the foot of the Cross via a retreat in a Trappist monastery in *En Route* (1895) and by living in Chartres in *The Cathedral* (1898) until he finally embraces Roman Catholicism in *The Oblate of St Benedict* (1903).

£7.99   ISBN 1 873982 57 7   304p   B.Format

Torture Garden – *Octave Mirbeau*

"A century after its first publication, this book is still capable of shocking. The opening satire is probably meaningful only to scholars of French political history, but the subsequent journey into the Far East accentuates connections between love and death, sex and depravity, fastidiousness and pleasure. And the petty, parochial corruptions of the narrator are put into context by the immersion into the Sadeian world of the *Torture Garden*."
   The Times

Oscar Wilde recommended *Torture Garden* to Frank Harris describing it as "revolting . . . a sort of grey adder."

"This hideously decadent *fin de siecle* novel by the French anarchist Mirbeau has become an underground classic. A cynical first half exposes the rottenness of politics, commerce and the *petit bourgeois*; in the second half, our totally corrupt narrator travels to China and meets the extraordinary Clara. She shows him the *Torture Garden*, a place of exotic flowers and baroque sadism. There are satirical and allegorical dimensions, but it remains irreducibly horrible."
   Phil Baker in *The Sunday Times*

£7.99   ISBN 1 873982 53 4   210p   B.Format